"Wherever you find yourself—whether you're a victim, survivor, overcomer, or conqueror of domestic abuse—you'll find Gardner is a trustworthy guide on your journey to hope and healing. This book is immensely practical and deeply spiritual. Anyone who engages with the steps outlined here and does the hard work of processing what has happened to them will benefit. Please do yourself a favor and have your pen and journal handy when you begin. Then watch with expectation as God meets you right where you are and draws you along the path to where you were always meant to be."

ANNA LeBaron, author of *The Polygamist's Daughter: A Memoir*

"With compassion, wisdom, and a proper understanding of Scripture, Karen will convince you that God loves you more than he hates divorce. Let her lead you through the healing that awaits you as you trust God with your betrayal and pain. You will boldly face your future knowing that, as Karen writes, 'Your life will not be defined by what was done to you, but by what *God does* with what was done to you.'"

CINDI McMENAMIN, national speaker, Bible teacher, and author of seventeen books, including *When Women Walk Alone*

"God abhors evil and hates abuse toward his children. While the world heaps guilt, shame, and condemnation on those who have endured abuse, Karen DeArmond Gardner shares God's unconditional love. She understands that secrets no longer hold their power when they are exposed to the light. God has brought beauty from ashes as he has used Karen to speak up for others and show how she learned to live again after escaping an abusive marriage, and how you can have a voice too."

DR. MICHELLE L. BENGTSON, clinical neuropsychologist and award-winning author of *Hope Prevails*

T0311043

HOPE FOR HEALING FROM DOMESTIC ABUSE

HOPE FOR HEALING FROM DOMESTIC ABUSE

Reaching for God's Promise
of Real Freedom

KAREN DEARMOND GARDNER

KREGEL
PUBLICATIONS

Published in association with Cyle Young of C.Y.L.E. (Cyle Young Literary Elite, LLC), a literary agency.

Cataloging-in-Publication Data is on file with the Library of Congress.

ISBN 978-0-8254-4694-8, print
ISBN 978-0-8254-7742-3, epub

Printed in the United States of America
21 22 23 24 25 26 27 28 29 30 / 5 4 3 2 1

This book is dedicated to my mother, Virginia, my Moses.
Without her there wouldn't be a book.

To my children, who are proof that
God brings good out of hard.

And to my beloved husband, Tom, who shows
me every day that love is more than words,
and it's clear to all that he loves me well.

CONTENTS

Don't Stop, There's More . . .

FOREWORD

I've known Karen DeArmond Gardner for several years as a fellow author and member of the same writer's group and association. It is with great enthusiasm that I recommend *Hope for Healing from Domestic Abuse* as a must-read for those who have left an abusive relationship or are considering leaving one.

Karen is a woman of integrity, care, and passion. Her heart embraces others and their stories. She believes that women are stronger than they realize, so she speaks directly to them about abuse. Some may believe they can't relate to a book like *Hope for Healing from Domestic Abuse* because they didn't endure physical abuse. Karen asks, Are you waiting for the other shoe to drop? Have you ever thought, *If only I hadn't said that or did this, I wouldn't have been hit or verbally assaulted?* Or have you told yourself, *I can't leave because God hates divorce, and if I ended my marriage, I'd ruin my children's lives?*

I didn't endure physical abuse, but many years into my marriage I realized that I was experiencing emotional abuse. After becoming a licensed professional counselor and marriage and family therapist after my divorce, I was able to identify the emotional abuse and other subtle abuse I endured. In those early years, I always thought it was my fault because that's what I was told. I was hesitant to divorce because I was afraid of wearing the scarlet *D*. I didn't think I would be welcome in my church anymore, which wasn't true. It is difficult for many of us to admit to being abused, but our habits, our words, and even our lack of words reveal what we have experienced.

Karen may not have professional letters after her name that reflect academic training and work experience, but she has earned the degree of "lived and survived." She gives a well-balanced presentation of domestic abuse and what it takes not only to survive but also to be healed. She states facts, gives excellent examples, and takes the shame away when we find ourselves relating to her stories or facts. She not only survived thirty years of domestic violence, she's taken the steps to be truly healed from it. The reader will find this to be a cornerstone for the book: It's not only about surviving. It's about healing.

When she and I collaborated on writing this foreword, it became clear to her that I may still need some healing. I had admitted to her that I don't like the word *victim*. I struggled with it. Karen convinced me that we have to face the fact that we are/were victims. There is a difference between *being* a victim and *acting* like a victim. In my practice, some clients enjoy the victim role. I didn't want to be that person. Karen helped me embrace the word *victim* in a different way. There is truth in the word. Avoiding identifying with it doesn't help. It will tempt us not to get the help we need.

Karen helps those of us who have also experienced spiritual abuse by others misusing Scripture to minimize or dismiss our situation. Some churches and church members have, unfortunately, re-abused victims by quoting Scripture incorrectly or using it to shame them. They minimize our pain, shift the blame from the abuser to the victim, and ostracize us. *Hope for Healing from Domestic Abuse* includes encouraging, supportive, and accurate Scripture we can use to combat our own doubts as well as accusations from the enemy or from friends and family members.

As we live with abuse, "why" questions fill our minds. Why does God allow this abuse? Why does no one see my abuser's cruelty? Why wasn't I enough for him? Karen addresses these critical topics. She provides examples and suggestions of how to address these questions. She also addresses our fears, doubts, grief, and anger at God. She offers readers hope, courage, freedom, and ways to live in truth and reality.

Karen does one-on-one mentoring through word-of-mouth referrals. Since she can only see a small number of individuals, she felt God was calling her to write this book to reach larger numbers who need to read it and be mentored by her in this way. This book does not recommend divorce; it offers freedom of choice without shame.

God loves you more than he hates divorce. There is no doubt God hates divorce—so do I; so do many divorced people. Hating something doesn't mean it's prohibited; it means it has consequences that are unfortunate but also good. As a therapist, I hate divorce for what it does to us and to our families, but I hate abuse much more because of what it does to us and to our families. According to Karen, the hope we have is this: what the enemy would use to destroy us, God will use to heal us.

Laura McPherson, MS, LPC, LMF
Licensed Professional Counselor
Licensed Marriage and Family Therapist

LEAVING IS JUST THE BEGINNING

And I am certain that God, who began the good work within you, will continue his work until it is finally finished on the day when Christ Jesus returns.
—Philippians 1:6

You likely never thought you'd be reading a book on healing from domestic abuse. But here you are. And I'm glad you came. If you're like me, you may not know that you can heal from the trauma from abuse.

Notice this book is not called *Twelve Easy Steps to Heal from Domestic Abuse*. That's because there are no easy steps to this kind of healing, and there aren't just twelve. The journey to healing is long, arduous, wonderful, and scary all at the same time. Freedom isn't one and done. It's a process that you may have to fight for to keep.

Through the last sixteen-plus years of healing, I couldn't have imagined how deep God's love is for me. My hope is that you will discover the same depth of his love.

When I left my abuser, I purchased every book I could find to figure out what happened to me and how to deal with it. None of those books helped ease the pain or made me feel better. They did explain what happened to me, and it was shocking to discover names and definitions for everything I experienced. Since that time, I've discovered more words and better explanations.

Because of the type of churches I attended, I was taught life is hard, so endure until Jesus returns or until you die and go to heaven. I've since learned that's only part of the story. The Gospels tell us about Jesus, who offered living water (John 4:10) and called himself the bread of life (John 6:48).

Scripture tells us he's the God "who is able, through his mighty power at work within us, to accomplish infinitely more than we might ask or think" (Ephesians 3:20). And in John 10:10, Jesus said, "The thief comes only to steal and kill and destroy; I came that they would have life, and have it abundantly" (NASB).

You may believe that domestic violence will haunt you for the rest of your life, but I'm saying no. The verse at the beginning of this introduction states that God will work in you until the day he returns. The apostle Paul, who wrote that verse, was certain, persuaded, and convinced that God would keep his promise to complete what he started in you. God didn't save you to leave you wallowing in a pit of despair for a lifetime.

Do you, like me, long to know God's purpose and destiny for your life? I mistakenly thought *purpose* meant ministry and serving God through writing, speaking, being an artist, taking on a profession, or devoting myself to missions. I was wrong. Those are things we may do because we love him, but they are only part of our destiny. What is your destiny and mine? Reaching for God's promise. It sounds too simple, but it's not. His love for you and me is deeper than the ocean and wider than the universe.

Yet abuse distorts love, and love becomes a curse word—something to be given and taken away. Abuse turns love into a weapon instead of a sacrifice. My desire is for you to know and experience God's love.

God's love is multidimensional and limitless.

There are seventeen variations for the word *love* in the Hebrew and Greek: affection, beloved, words of love, friend, amorousness, compassion, desire, to choose, brotherly, sisterly, husband and wife, benevolence, greedy love, love toward children, tenderness, devotion, and passion.[1] Most of the words have more than one meaning.

God's love is multidimensional and limitless. That kind of love will get you through whatever your enemy, Satan, throws at you. God's love for you is more—additionally, again, also, besides, either, further, furthermore, for good measure, into the bargain, on top of, greater—than the abuse or anything the evil one or your abuser throws at you.

Why am I bringing up love? When you've lived in and survived abuse, love seems foreign and uncharacteristic and beyond comprehension, which makes it difficult for you to receive anything from others, especially love. As you create new friendships with women and men, you'll find it easier to give than to receive kindness and love. And it's even harder to ask for help when you need it. Asking for help may make you feel weak. Yet opening yourself up for help is not weakness. It is an act of strength.

My hope is that you will discover day after day the depths of God's love for you and that it will transform your life, giving you the courage to change your world.

Throughout this book, I'll use the term *BeLoved*. It is who you are. You can read it several ways: *be loved* (live as one who is loved mightily) and *beloved* (one who is highly loved). It's a term of affection, devotion, and love.

My hope as you read the words, sentences, paragraphs, pages, and chapters is that you'll discover there is freedom and abundance after abuse. And I pray you'll also discover that God loves you more than he hates divorce, more than he hates abuse, more that he hates anything.

I invite you to join me on a journey through pain and trauma and into the *more* God has for you as you ride the roller coaster called healing and wholeness.

At the end of each chapter, you'll find a section called "Reaching for More," which is designed to help you put words to what happened to you, start conversations with Jesus, and discover there is more to life than living in pain and agony. Read the book, and when you are ready, grab your Bible and journal, review each chapter, and complete the questions at the end of the chapter. Take your time. Healing begins as you interact with the Father, Jesus, and the Holy Spirit.

PART 1

VICTIM

We Have to Start Someplace

You may say, "I am not a victim! I refuse to be called a victim." I can understand those feelings. But acknowledging you are a victim says you recognize that you were hurt, maligned, deceived, and abused. It's what happened to you, not who you are.

As you begin your journey toward wholeness, let's look at what you have survived. As you revisit some tender places in your soul, keep in mind that you are not alone. Jesus knew betrayal too: "He was despised and rejected—a man of sorrows, acquainted with deepest grief. We turned our backs on him and looked the other way. He was despised, and we did not care" (Isaiah 53:3).

CHAPTER 1

UNFALTERING

When It's Time to Take Your Life Back

*By your mighty power I can walk through any devastation,
and you will keep me alive, reviving me. Your power set
me free from the hatred of my enemies.*

—Psalm 138:7 (TPT)

After a long day at work, I settled into my favorite chair to watch mindless television and avoid talking to my then husband. Finding myself bored with TV, I began to flip through the latest edition of *Today's Christian Woman* magazine.[2] I felt as if someone plunged a hot poker into my heart as I read that God doesn't condone abuse, that I was one in four women.

I sneaked a glance at Guy, trying not to react, afraid he somehow knew what I was reading. *Can he read my mind?* As I continued reading the article, "The Silent Epidemic," *shock* is the only word that describes how it felt to see my life played out in print. How could they know about the physical and verbal abuse? Yet that wasn't what stopped my heart. It was the author talking about husbands destroying sentimental property, issuing death threats, and isolating their wives from family and friends.

The harsh reality smacked me in the face.

My husband was an abuser.

It's not just the way he was. It wasn't just because I made him angry. *He was a predator.* It meant our marriage was a travesty. Even harder to admit . . . if he was an abuser, *I was abused.*

I couldn't be.

Oh, but I was.

I'd been in denial for thirty years. To accept it, to say it out loud made it too real. I needed to leave him, but fear screamed, *You can't leave—he won't let you.*

Oh, dear God! What have I done? It was as if I woke from a stupor. *Why did I assume I had to stay?*

Admitting your husband is an abuser is painful; it's admitting that maybe he doesn't love you, and you begin to question whether you love him. The revelation creates anxiety throughout your body as you wonder what to do next. You may falter between awakening and denial, which is understandable.

One year earlier, on our twenty-ninth anniversary, Guy assaulted me with cruel words and with his fists. When he finished, he shoved me out the door. Battered and bruised, I stumbled away from the house. My son picked me up and we drove two hours to my daughter's home in another state.

I stayed away for a month, but once again, Guy "got right with Jesus," admitted what he did, and lost his career in law enforcement. Guilt told me I should stand by my man. But everything in me fought going back. The thought made me sick. Yet I did go back. After all, he took responsibility and changed. For nine months, he was a changed man . . . until he wasn't.

Cascades of despair rolled over me as I continued reading the article. I avoided looking at him. I couldn't let him see. He must suspect nothing. My enduring what Guy had done wasn't God's purpose for our marriage. God isn't okay with abuse . . . of any kind.

Sitting on the other side of the room watching TV, he was unaware his world had just blown up. All the while, I was on a roller coaster of emotions, ranging from rage to terror.

With every plan I made to leave, fear rose to remind me who I was. Shattered. Worthless. Conquered. Hopeless. But how would I get out?

In the abuse dynamic, there's an invisible line. If you cross it, you pay his price. His generosity determines if you eat, if you drive the car, what you wear, where you sleep, or *if* you sleep. I could have left, you say. I could've called the police, you may reason. But my husband *was* the police and, above all else, I'd been taught that God hates divorce.

As I read that article, in that moment I knew it wasn't me. It was him.

I was done—done pretending, done denying, done being treated as if I was nothing to him.

Have you had your defining moment? The moment you knew it wasn't you—that it was him and that he may never change?

Your defining moment is important; it helps you to remain unfaltering when you may be wavering about whether to stay or go.

> Have you had your defining moment? The moment you knew it wasn't you—that it was him and that he may never change?

Once I decided I was done, God immediately started to put my rescue into motion. Do I wonder why God took so long to answer me? Absolutely. But I could never have orchestrated the miracle he was about to work.

THE ESCAPE

As winter approached and Christmas drew near, I began preparing for my daughter's college graduation, which was the week before Christmas. My mother was coming to visit, and I hadn't seen my mom in years! Both excitement and apprehension overwhelmed me. The weeks leading up to Mom's visit were a roller coaster of ups and downs between silence and anger, followed by verbal jabs, blame, and control. Guy ordered me not to allow my mom to come. I refused. This wasn't about us. It was about my mother watching her granddaughter graduate from college.

The time leading up to her visit was like wandering through a mine field. No matter which way I turned or stepped, I was bound to land on one. While mom and I helped to set up for my daughter's graduation party, Guy left for home, which was two hours away. No warning, no words, just up and left without mom and me, leaving us to get a ride home with my son.

After graduation, the days leading up to Christmas were hell on earth. Mom and I would take off each day to shop, while I battled indecision. Should I leave him? Should I not? The answer *should* have been obvious, but it clearly wasn't. Mom would give advice, but wouldn't choose for me, and each night Mom packed my clothes, expecting I would leave.

Choosing to leave aroused distress, a sense of impending danger, dread, and apprehension. It's understandable why so many abused women may waver between staying and going. But I told myself, "Take a deep breath and choose you." It's advice I still give to other women in my situation.

Terror overwhelmed me as I thought of the repercussions of leaving. I sincerely believed I would disappoint God. After all, he hates divorce, right? Yet I knew, deep in my soul, God was nudging me to leave. But in my panic, the voice of fear sounded more persuasive than the voice of God.

Christmas 2004 went down as both my worst and best Christmas. It was the day I stopped the yo-yo of indecision and determined to stop dancing around my husband's core of darkness and leave.

After my mom and our adult children went to bed, he and I stayed up. Not to savor the quiet around the tree but for him to pound me with his words. For hours, he barraged me with all my failings and what he would do if I ever cheated or left him. It took everything in me to not laugh, knowing in a few short hours I would leave. If I drifted off, he'd startle me, act like he would hit me. As he raged, the Holy Spirit whispered, *Tell him to stop in Jesus's name.* But my fear of this man was stronger than my faith in the Holy Spirit.

By three in the morning, his rage spent, he demanded sex—his final act of humiliation and dominance. My body yielded to his and betrayed me. He fell asleep as if nothing had happened. It was his normal pattern. I was flooded with rage, humiliation, and shame. I'd waffled between staying and leaving for a week. Now I was determined to leave this man. Sleep eluded me as I bounced between dread and excitement at finally being free.

The Sunday morning sun woke me. For a moment I lay there praying Guy wouldn't wake up. Quaking with fear and apprehension, I slid out of bed, took one last look at him, and prayed, "Please God, don't let him wake up," as I slipped out of the room. I walked out the door, not to church, but to freedom. Fear mocked me as my mom and I loaded our luggage into the trunk. I was doing this. Leaving, not on a jet plane, but in a Monte Carlo. As we shut the car doors, I turned the key, expecting to hear the roar of an engine. Instead, we were met with silence. Total and complete silence.

In a flash, my hope was as dead as the engine. I jumped out of the car, crying, yanking luggage out of the trunk. There would be no escape today—until the voice of my seventy-two-year-old mother penetrated my fear: "Karen. Karen! We'll call a tow truck."

We found a safe place to wait, and my rescuing knight drove up in his shiny white tow truck to save the day. "I'm running away from home," I said. "You must not wake him." As my fairy godmother and knight drove off to recharge the Monte, I waited at the 7-Eleven, expecting Guy to show up. My heart leapt when my mother drove up.

As we drove to Texas, hope soared. *I'm free!*

I remember feeling surprised that I actually left him. I now know I was feeling courageous. How did you feel when you left? Scared? Courageous? Both and everything in between?

> I remember feeling surprised that I actually left him. I now know I was feeling courageous.

YOU DID WHAT?

After my successful escape, my mom didn't want me to leave Texas and go back to my job, even though I wasn't going back to my husband. But I felt as if I couldn't leave my employer without any notice. As soon as I returned to work, I knew I'd made a huge mistake. I didn't realize how hard it would be to leave a place I thought was home. But this place was no longer my home.

I struggled with indecision. Should I stay in this city I'd called home for thirty years or move to Texas? Each day the terror inside me grew until I knew it was time to put in my notice at work. You'd think leaving would be a no-brainer. But this brain was in a massive state of confusion.

I spoke to Guy twice on the phone, January 9 and 16. I told him I wasn't coming back and that we both needed counseling. I suggested that maybe, just maybe we could put our marriage back together. Did I really want to put our marriage back together? Did I really think counseling would help? I didn't. I appeased him with hope where there wasn't any. He seemed calm. I let my guard down and talked about visiting friends moving to Alaska. It proved a massive mistake.

I was on my way home after visiting my friends when I spotted his unmistakable '72 blue and white Chevy truck several car lengths behind me. My heart slammed into my chest as fear flooded my body.

Hoping it was a coincidence and he didn't see me, yet knowing it wasn't, I exploded with fear when the light turned red. Stuck in traffic, my hands shaking, I tried to remember how to lock the doors.

Sweet relief hit as I heard the click of doors locking . . . just as he pulled the handle.

Looking into his face, a face I hadn't seen for twenty-four days, sent bone-chilling shivers up my spine. He wanted to talk but there were no words he could say, promises he could make, or actions he could take to change my mind. I no longer wanted to be with him. The veil had lifted, and I saw the monster within. He didn't love me. I was his possession. His drug of choice. Was I afraid of him? Absolutely.

Anger and frustration contorted his face as he demanded we talk. With my every refusal, he became angrier, louder, and more insistent. The exchange lasted for what seemed like an eternity. The moment the light turned green I sped away, leaving him standing in traffic. All rational thought left as panic took over.

Getting away was my only thought. As he chased me through the city, a reasonable person would call 911 or drive to the police station. But I was beyond rational thought. Instead, I called my daughter, who lives two hours away and was unable to help. Imagine answering that call, expecting to chat and all you hear is your mother screaming. Though she was an adult and married, that night traumatized her as much as it did me.

With no destination in mind I drove for eight miles through the city, begging God to do something, anything, to stop him. As the sun dipped out of sight and darkness surrounded me I lost all hope.

If you ever leave, if you ever cheat . . .

I. Will. Kill. You.

The words stuck in my head, playing repeatedly, consuming me with terror.

In the last year and a half, he'd lost everything, including both his career in law enforcement and his wife.

He had nothing left to lose.

I had everything to lose.

At one point, Guy slammed into my car and ran me off the road. Rage boiled out of him as he charged my car, and attempted to break through my window with his elbow. Jolted by my daughter's voice, I followed her instructions. "Hang up, Mom. Call 911!"

As I punched the numbers into the phone, he stood next to my car and said, almost resigned, "You're calling the cops?" Duh!

If looks could kill, he would have died on the spot. Deflated, his rage spent, he walked back to his truck and drove down the block to wait for the police.

Two officers came to my rescue; one spoke to Guy while the other interviewed me. The officer asked me if this had ever happened before. Shame washed over me. How do I explain a lifetime of abuse after thirty years of keeping the family secret? A million thoughts ran through my mind. As I looked up at the officer, he repeated his question, "Has this happened before?"

"Yes."

"Do you want me to arrest him?"

I thought, *He would be so mad.*

Why in the world did it matter if he was mad? To this day, my one regret of that night is not having him arrested. He deserved at least one night in jail. I only considered how he would react, instead of thinking of my own safety.

"No, I'm leaving tomorrow. I'm moving to Texas. And I'm never coming back." The officer asked me again if I was sure and if I had a place to go, assuring me they would keep him there until I left.

I was shaking and crying as I drove away from my nightmare. Eventually, mile after mile, my hope returned.

I don't remember all the thoughts that were racing through my mind during my flight to Texas the next day. However, I *do* remember my constant companions—fear and shame—tagging along, arms looped through mine. They had found a friend, and they weren't about to let go.

Texas became my place of safety and Psalm 107:1–9 my anthem:

Give thanks to the LORD, for he is good!
    His faithful love endures forever.
Has the LORD redeemed you? Then speak out!
    Tell others he has redeemed you from your enemies.
For he has gathered the exiles from many lands,
    from east and west,
    from north and south.

Some wandered in the wilderness,
    lost and homeless.
Hungry and thirsty,
    they nearly died.
"LORD, help!" they cried in their trouble,
    and he rescued them from their distress.
He led them straight to safety,
    to a city where they could live.
Let them praise the LORD for his great love
    and for the wonderful things he has done for them.
For he satisfies the thirsty
    and fills the hungry with good things.

January 19, 2005, is my Independence Day—a day I thought I would never see and a day far beyond my imagination.

It was a "Pinch me, I'm dreaming" moment.

But it was no dream. I woke up in an unfamiliar place, surrounded by family I hadn't been around in thirty years. The weight of shame enveloped me as I walked down the stairs to face my family at breakfast the next morning. I was clothed but I felt naked and exposed.

IS THIS ALL THERE IS?

Admitting you are or were abused is one of the hardest things you'll do. It's horrifying to say the words out loud: "My husband is an abuser." I understand the pain you may be experiencing right now as you're reading. Seeing him for who he is or was means seeing yourself for who you have become. Once you acknowledge you are a victim, you can do something about it.

Your journey to healing can begin today. . . . Jesus will guide each step you take.

If you're still in your marriage, you can plan your escape. If you're out, you can plan to stay out. Did you know it takes most of us abused wives somewhere between six to eight times of repeated leaving before we finally leave for good? Each time we go back, he'll escalate. Precious one, your journey to healing can begin today. This place you may be in now is temporary. Jesus will guide each step you take toward healing.

ENCOUNTER GOD

Come, my BeLoved, on a journey to healing. I'm so sorry for what your abuser did to you. I will carry you as you read. I will fan the flame of hope within you. I am as close as your breath. You can face anything because I am with you. I heard your cries in the night, curled up, lost in hopelessness. I was there holding you, comforting you. Come with me, precious one, and you'll discover I am more than you ever imagined.

‑Your Comforter and Protector
(Psalm 116; Ephesians 3:20)

REACHING FOR MORE

Choosing to leave an abusive marriage is by far one of the most difficult decisions you made. You had a moment when the darkness lifted, what was obscure became clear, when the cloud lifted and you could finally see the hidden. Putting words to this moment will help you to remain unfaltering in your decision.

1. What were the circumstances that led up to your moment when you knew you were done?
2. How did those circumstances shift your thinking?
3. Identify and name the emotions that rose up in this process.
4. What was the decision you made in this moment, and how did you feel when you made it?
5. What is one thing you can do to remain unfaltering in your decision?

CHAPTER 2

UNDISGUISED

How Could You Know How Much Darkness Lived in Him?

But the wicked walk in thick darkness, like those who travel in fog, and yet don't have a clue why they keep stumbling!
—Proverbs 4:19 (TPT)

They lie awake at night to hatch their evil plots, always planning their schemes of darkness, and never once do they consider the evil of their ways.
—Psalm 36:4 (TPT)

How could I have known how much darkness lived in my ex-husband? How can we know how much darkness lives inside another? It's not like darkness is scrawled across their forehead. They don't have horns. They are charming, friendly, funny, and sweet. Do *they* even know how much darkness lurks inside them? It seems as if the words "I do" release the monster within.

While Guy and I dated, I did not understand how deep self-hatred was ingrained in his soul or how it would play out in our marriage. That factor alone gave the enemy fuel to forge a wildfire of bitterness, hostility, cruelty. Bitterness creates antagonism, which produces hostility, which turns into hatred, and reveals the cruelty buried within a person. It's impossible to develop love in this environment. It twists your character into a putrid place. Proverbs 4:23 states, "Guard your heart above all else, for it determines the course of your life." What lives in our hearts eventually flows out of our mouths.

When we married, Guy would manage his rage, but over time, the rage controlled him, demanding to be released. Between explosions of rage, covert cruelty disguised as jokes, mockery, and put-downs played out in our everyday life. When his pain became too heavy to bear, my compassion would kick in and I would carry the weight of his pain. I didn't realize abusers use this tactic to make you responsible for their pain. You may think it's biblical based on Galatians 6:2, which reads, "Share each other's burdens, and in this way obey the law of Christ." It seems like the right thing to do as a "good Christian wife," doesn't it? But God never intended for us to be responsible for another's pain.

Guy's burden became a horrendous taskmaster and started a pattern I couldn't break. Some might speculate that they would never allow someone to have that kind of control in their life, and early in my marriage, I would have agreed with them. But when these patterns are developing, you don't recognize you're in trouble until it's too late and it has turned into a way of life. You become like a lobster, slowly cooked in a kettle of cool water that becomes warmer and warmer until it boils. The poor lobster doesn't realize he died the moment he was placed in the kettle, and he doesn't even know he should get out.

Depending on your guy, at some point he may have shifted all the blame on you until you believed the darkness was in you. Nothing could be his fault so he makes you responsible for his darkness. When Guy cheated on me, he accused me of cheating on him. Such accusations continued with different scenarios throughout the marriage until I carried the blame for everything that went wrong.

REVEALING THE EVIL

How do you explain to someone, especially your family, what evil looks like? When all they may have seen is his generosity, humor, charm, and kindness? Even if they did experience his sullen moods, they may not equate his moodiness as abuse, or know to look deeper to see what is truly going on behind your closed doors.

You may not have words to explain what's happened to you, and they may think you're exaggerating because they think they know him. Family and friends only see what he wants them to see. You alone are privy to his true nature.

You are the one who takes the brunt of his meanness, unkindness, greed, selfishness, malice, put-downs, and ugliness. He demands subservience, his way or no way. He blames you for his behavior, withholds, and accuses. Eventually he controls every area of your life.

It may take months or years to fully comprehend all the abuse you endured at the hands of the one who should have loved you.

EXPOSE THE ABUSE

Over the first few weeks after I left Guy, the years of silence exploded as stories and horrors poured out of me. Rage became my outlet as I revealed thirty years of secrets.

Family: "Why didn't you tell us?"

Me: "Why didn't you ask?"

You. Never. Asked.

Not that I would have admitted the family secret if they had asked. Shame and pride had been duct tape over my mouth and soul. Their questions when I revealed the situation felt like condemnation, but when I talked with my sister-in-law fourteen years later, she said that their guilt was doing the asking. If they had only known, they could have done something.

During the years of my marriage, my family only knew what I told them, which wasn't much. So when I finally told them what had really been going on, their reaction shocked me. I knew my marriage was awful, but their faces said it was worse than awful.

Over the first six months after I left Guy, I gained clarity about what had happened to me. I realized that the man I'd married was a monster. With clarity came anger.

Why the h—— did I stay so long?

I was overwhelmed with feelings of stupidity, regret, and shame. "I kicked myself for my stupidity! I was thoroughly ashamed" (Jeremiah 31:19). That verse became my chorus. Hear me on this: just because we feel stupid for falling for an abuser doesn't mean we *are* stupid. There are scientific studies about how trauma damages our frontal lobe, the part of our brains that processes decisions and fight-or-flight reflexes. The frontal lobe houses our emotions, reasoning, planning, movement, and parts of speech. It is also involved in purposeful acts such as creativity, judgment, problem-solving, and planning.[3]

It's painful to admit that the man who promised to love you didn't recognize the definition of the word, much less know how to love. He created an environment of torment, isolation, silence, emotional and verbal abuse, control, and manipulation. And we fell for it.

Who wants to say that out loud for all to hear? I didn't.

Once I pulled my finger out of the dam, nothing could stem the flood of resentment, pain, and rage at him for what he did. At myself, for what I thought I allowed. *Poor, pitiful Karen. Her husband treated her so dreadfully. What's wrong with her? Why did she stay? I wouldn't put up with it for five minutes.*

The maxim "Hindsight is twenty-twenty" may be annoying, but it's true. Through the questions of others, I was finally beginning to see how awful things had really been. It was then that my own questions began battering me.

Why I married him is a question I still can't fully answer.

This may sound ludicrous, but I felt as if I didn't have a choice. Once I agreed to his marriage proposal, it never occurred to me I could change my mind and not marry him. Isn't it a woman's right to change her mind?

Guy was the first man to show me attention. He pursued me as no one had ever done. I won't bother you with the details of my lackluster dating life prior to meeting him. Let me just say his attention dazzled me. I thought this was love.

Until recently I attributed my brokenness to why he was drawn to me. Then a dear friend suggested another reason. He chose me because I'm empathetic, merciful, and see the best in people. I condemned myself for being broken, passive, and weak. But he saw the good in me; the essence of who I was is what attracted him

> He saw the good in me; the essence of who I was is what attracted him to me and why he latched on to me.

to me and why he latched on to me. His pursuit was over the top; he really let me know how much he liked me.

As he pulled me in, he covertly pushed my boundaries to see how far he could push me until I moved my boundary. When it was too far, he would pour out flattery to camouflage and distract me from seeing his ugly side. He would also remind me how much he loved me. He created a sandwich of flattery, ugliness, and flattery to disguise his true self.

This is what abusers and narcissists do. They target you and pull you into their web just like a spider draws in a fly. Once you're caught, it's hard to break free.

At what point do you realize you messed up? Sadly for me I'm not sure anymore.

WHY DID I STAY IN THE MARRIAGE?

Why did we stay? It may take years to answer that question. But simply understanding what kept us in the marriage doesn't bring relief, and it can often leave us feeling resentment and regret.

From the outset, Guy conditioned me to think only about him, his desires, his wants. He constantly reminded me not to ruin his name by airing our family secrets. Fear is a powerful controller. If I responded in a way he didn't like, he would hurt me enough that I would never want to do it again. I would do anything to avoid the pain, whether the pain was physical, verbal, or emotional.

They call this conditioning *trauma bonding.* Some would say I was codependent. However, codependency implies the victims are somehow at fault for another person's behavior and choices. We may think we can save them, not knowing that is part of the conditioning to keep us tied to the relationship. Most abusers follow similar patterns. They see someone kind, attentive, and loving, and they desire that person for themselves. Unfortunately, they are unable to create good bonds, and slowly, quietly they twist relationships and people until the victims are unrecognizable. This twisting is not the victim's fault.

Say it out loud: "It's not my fault. I didn't cause him to abuse me."

Say it out loud: "It's not my fault. I didn't cause him to abuse me." The fault is all his.

Your "picker" isn't broken. You didn't choose the wrong man. He was deliberate in choosing you. You may go to church and not believe in divorce. You've been taught to forgive, submit, and not complain.

You may have survived childhood abuse, which could mean you were already conditioned to abuse. You may have thought you were dating, when in reality he was grooming you with kindness and love for what was to come after you said, "I do." You married him not knowing the darkness

Domestic violence is not the same thing as suffering for Jesus.

lurking beneath the facade he showed in public. His darkness is not your fault. Throughout my Christian life, I heard all the messages about not giving up too soon on God's promises. My pastor would talk about the woman married to a mean man. She would pray for him and ultimately he would come to Jesus. What I heard was, "Don't give up on him or your marriage; your promise is right around the corner." So I would hang on, waiting for a promise that never came through.

I thought I was suffering for Jesus by staying in an abusive marriage. Let me state this very clearly: Domestic violence is not the same thing as suffering for Jesus. It isn't a "light momentary affliction" as described in 2 Corinthians 4:17 (ESV) or referred to in verses like James 1:12, "God blesses those who patiently endure testing and temptation. Afterward they will receive the crown of life that God has promised to those who love him."

We're not enduring for Jesus so that praying harder, longer, on our knees, on our face, in our living room, or on the bathroom floor will change someone who doesn't think they need to change. I believed if I prayed the right words or formula, Guy would come to Jesus and the nightmare would end.

I presumed the state of my marriage was retribution for not seeking God's leading about whether I should marry Guy. Since I married him, I had to remain with him. I thought I was suffering for Jesus.

I also had hope he would change. In the beginning of our marriage, long periods of time passed between outbursts. There was no way of perceiving what would set him off. It could be a meal he didn't like, leaving him so I could visit my family, saying the wrong thing, doing the wrong thing. He was the only one who could establish what the *thing* was. He rarely said he was sorry. Once the crisis was over, he acted as if nothing had transpired. Life would go back to what I thought was normal. I lived for the in-between seasons when he was kind, caring, and funny. As the outbursts occurred more often, I would walk around on eggshells. Ultimately, the eggshells turned into land mines. Then the cycle of silence, madness, verbal and emotional abuse, maybe physical abuse, sex to reestablish his dominance, and peace would begin again.

But with an abuser, peace really isn't peace; abuse becomes subtle and covert. The abuse rarely stops, it just looks different from the outbursts of rage. My friend Elsa calls it the faces of abuse. You never know which face you'll see on any given day.

Beyond that, all the details of escape were overwhelming. How did I plan when I had no place to go? Did I call the police? He was the police. There weren't any shelters in my area. Call my family? They were fifteen hundred miles away. Shame and pride told me I couldn't tell my family or anyone else.

Honestly, I had a million excuses, but when it came right down to it . . . I was petrified. Fear was the motivating force holding me in the marriage. I couldn't plan because I couldn't dream. I couldn't see life any different from what it was, which left me hopeless.

One of the biggest obstacles for me? How much God hates divorce. He does, but not for the reasons we expect. I also discovered God hates abuse.

HOW DOES GOD FEEL ABOUT ABUSE?

Let's look at what the Scriptures say about abuse:

> There are six evils God truly hates and a seventh that is an
>   abomination to him:
> Putting others down while considering yourself superior,
> spreading lies and rumors,

spilling the blood of the innocent,
plotting evil in your heart toward another,
gloating over doing what's plainly wrong,
spouting lies in false testimony,
and stirring up strife between friends [and spouses].
These are entirely despicable to God! (Proverbs 6:16–19 TPT)

That sounds like the very definition of verbal and emotional abuse. "Walk away from an angry man or you'll embrace a snare in your soul by becoming bad-tempered just like him" (Proverbs 22:24 TPT).

The book of Proverbs refers to abusers as fools. In Hebrew a fool[4] is described this way: a fool despises wisdom and discipline (1:7; 15:5); makes fun of guilt (14:9); is quarrelsome, contentious, and argumentative (20:3); is sexually unrestrained, lascivious, and lewd (6:31–33); goes beyond proper bounds, is unrestrained by law or morality, and disregards rules (5:22–23); and makes it useless—absurd, costly, unwise—to invest your time in instructing him (16:22; 27:22).

Here are a few other verses from Proverbs:

"Fools think their own way is right" (12:15).
"Associate with fools and get in trouble" (13:20).
"Escape quickly from the company of fools; they're a waste of your
time, a waste of your words" (14:7 MSG).
"The fool only deceives himself and refuses to face reality. Fools
mock the need for repentance" (14:8–9 TPT).

Why was it okay for David to run and hide from his tormentor, yet abused wives today are advised to stay . . . and pray more?

Hundreds of verses in the Bible deal with abuse. Proverbs 31:8 reminds us, "Speak up for those who cannot speak for themselves; ensure justice for those being crushed." This is why I'm cracking the silence on domestic violence. While we want God to put a stop to the violence, it rarely occurs to us that he will use us to be the ones to speak up for others.

For me, talking to my family started me on my healing journey. By cracking the silence on our family secret, a light shined into the darkness of my soul. Take heart in the promise: "The light shines in the darkness, and the darkness can never extinguish it" (John 1:5).

Hear David's lament in Psalm 55:12–14, 20–21:

> It is not an enemy who taunts me—I could bear that. It is not my foes who so arrogantly insult me—I could have hidden from them. Instead, it is you—my equal, my companion and close friend. What good fellowship we once enjoyed as we walked together to the house of God. . . .
>
> As for my companion, he betrayed his friends; he broke his promises. His words are as smooth as butter, but in his heart is war. His words are as soothing as lotion, but underneath are daggers!

Why was it okay for David to run and hide from his tormentor, yet abused wives today are advised to stay, be submissive and respectful, give him more sex, be a better wife, and pray more?

The answer is God doesn't *expect* us to stay. If a stranger kidnapped you, violated and abused you, the judge would condemn him to prison. He wouldn't advise you to welcome the intruder into your home, to live with him, sleep with him, be kind to him so he would change and develop into a better man. Yet many people expect us to invite our abusers back into our lives when they say, "I'm sorry."

DON'T LOSE HOPE

You may feel hopeless and lost in a sea of misery. But, dear one, there is hope. God doesn't just tell us to be hopeful. He is hope. It's his nature. It's who he is. It doesn't matter if you don't see it or can't feel it. Hope is all we have and will get us through.

As you read my paraphrase of Psalm 124, be saturated with hope.

A Song of Hope
What if the Lord had not been on my side?
Say it again dear one:

What if the Lord had not been on my side when my husband
   turned on me and attacked?
I would have been swallowed alive by his violent anger as if
   caught in a flood, the raging waters smashing me against
   the debris, pulling me under. Just when I could not hold
   my breath any longer, up I would come for a precious
   breath of air only to be sucked under the water once again.
   Pulled along by the fury of his rage.
Bless the Lord, Oh my soul!
You did not let me be torn apart by the teeth of his rage.
I escaped, ran for my life, set free from his trap. The trap is
   broken, and I am free!
Thank you, Oh God. You who made heaven and earth, you
   are my rescuer and protector.

Psalm 5:9 reads: "Their words are unreliable. Destruction is in
their hearts, drawing people into their darkness with their speeches.
They are smooth-tongued deceivers, flattering with their words" (TPT).
(The last sentence is translated in the New American Standard Bible
as "Their throat is an open grave; they flatter with their tongue.")

BeLoved, don't blame yourself for not seeing his darkness. He
worked hard to protect his image and disguise the darkness, even with
God's name on his lips. Isaiah 29:13 says it this way, "These people
say they are mine. They honor me with their lips, but their hearts
are far from me. And their worship of me is nothing but man-made
rules learned by rote." The note on the verse says the Greek version
reads, "Their worship is a farce." You may think God doesn't see, but
he absolutely knows what is in your abuser's heart.

ENCOUNTER GOD

*BeLoved, I am in you, filling you with comfort and strength as
you unravel all you've endured. I translate your pain into words*

and intercede for you before the Father. I reveal truth to you, teach you, and remind you of the Father's love for you.

-Your Advocate, the Holy Spirit
(Ephesians 5:18–20; Isaiah 51:12;
Romans 8:26–27; John 14:17, 26)

REACHING FOR MORE

The disguise has been removed, you see him for who he really is and understand that he has no intention of changing. You may begin questioning how you could have been so fooled by him. If you can, close your eyes and think back to when you were dating as you respond to the next questions.

1. What was it like when you first met him? Was he charming and disarming?
2. How did you feel when you were with him?
3. How did you feel when you weren't with him?
4. How did he push your boundaries and how did he make you think it was your choice to break your boundaries?
5. When did he remove his disguise and what was your reaction?

CHAPTER 3

UNENCHANTED

When Your Nightmare Is Disguised as a Fairy Tale

*This man's name was Nabal, and his wife, Abigail, was a
sensible and beautiful woman. But Nabal, a descendant
of Caleb, was crude and mean in all his dealings.*
—1 Samuel 25:3

As women, we long to find love. Deep inside we want to experience
the fairy tale. It's exhilarating when we're pursued and romanced.

But what happens when the fairy tale turns into a nightmare?
How do we redefine normal and escape the nightmare that torments
us in the light of day?

I wonder when Abigail, the woman in the verse above, discovered
she was in a nightmare. I'm sure Nabal saw Abigail's beauty and poise
when he met her. The story in the Bible doesn't tell us how they met.
We assume it was an arranged marriage. Was he handsome? Kind?
From Scripture we know Abigail was diligent, kind, resourceful, and
a peacemaker. Did Nabal keep his cruelty hidden until he and Abigail
were married? Or did Abigail know the kind of man she was marrying
before she said "I do"?

Did Nabal struggle keeping his meanness in, or did it ooze out?

In Bible times, women had no choice, voice, or recourse about
whom they married. Men had absolute authority in the marriage. A
wife couldn't leave her husband or seek a divorce. She was bound to
him until he died or he decided he no longer wanted her.

Abigail amazes me. She kept her dignity in spite of Nabal's
attempts to break her. When Nabal refused to help David and his
men, Abigail bravely acted, gathering provisions for David and his

men. She took the blame for her husband's behavior. She knew if she didn't, she and all her servants would be dead. I believe when David encountered Abigail, he immediately recognized her humility, strength, and dignity. I imagine he saw himself in her. Both of them knew the pain of betrayal and the need to fight for survival. David rescued Abigail and provided her with a safe place to live the rest of her life after Nabal dropped dead. (I encourage you to read the full story in 1 Samuel 25.)

WHAT'S NORMAL?

We all want normal. But what defines normal? Normal implies common, regular, and ordinary. When it comes to our childhood and background, I'm sure my definition of normal was different from yours. But we would each say our childhood was normal, even if normal was ugly. Chances are the details of your upbringing shaped your idea of normal as it did mine. What shaped my normal?

According to my mother, I was a carefree, fun-loving child until age ten, when I was molested. I changed from being a happy, carefree child into a guarded, closed-off child.

Within six months of that incident, my mother remarried. Without warning, a new daddy showed up to live with us.

As a teen all I wanted was to be liked and wanted. I hid behind a facade of people pleasing. I didn't date much. Boys only seemed to like me when we were at a party. In the light of day, they didn't want to be seen with me.

Shortly after I turned fifteen, my mother started dragging my siblings and me to church—Sunday morning, Sunday night, and Wednesday night. I hated every minute of it.

About the same time we started attending church, I started taking drugs. For almost two years my world revolved around getting high, drinking, partying, and going to church.

I believed God was mean and exacting, waiting to strike me down. I had no desire to go to hell, but I was having too much fun to buy into this Jesus stuff. I equated Jesus with boring.

Two months before my seventeenth birthday, I heard about a different Jesus—a Jesus who wanted to give me more, a "high" drugs couldn't give. I asked Jesus into my life. I can still feel the peace that pushed out the chaos.

I graduated high school and then Bible college, after which my plan was to spend the summer in California with my family before moving to Chicago to be a missionary for a messianic ministry.

Once home, a high school friend introduced me to Guy. He was relentless in his pursuit of me. And that was a first for this girl, who hadn't dated much through high school and college. After three days, Guy said he loved me and kissed me goodnight. *How do you know? It's only been three days*, I thought. Confused, I asked my mom, "How do you know you're in love?" I don't remember her response, though I remember she looked surprised. It all seemed surreal.

Guy would show up at the house to pick me up with his car stereo blaring "I Want to Marry You" over and over from his eight-track tape player. His pursuit meant he loved me, that I was headed into a fairy tale, right?

We met and married within two and a half months. What was I thinking? Apparently, I wasn't. It never occurred to me I could jump off the train. I said "I do" and thought I was beginning the fairy tale of being loved and adored, starting to build a new life. Isn't that what we all desire? Instead, my fairy tale slowly turned into a nightmare from which I couldn't awaken. There

My fairy tale slowly turned into a nightmare from which I couldn't awaken.

were so many red flags I didn't know to pay attention to. I later learned the over-the-top nature of Guy's pursuit is called "love-bombing." It's a classic grooming technique to keep you from seeing the red flags.

What he called "love" morphed into punishment, pain, hurt, rejection, abandonment, being ignored, and feeling unprotected and used. "Love" had been completely distorted. Love wasn't beautiful, warm, or fuzzy anymore. It became a game of manipulation, blame, and control.

I was young when my father left, so I didn't remember his abuse of my mother. I blocked out the memories, but the lingering effects were there. What I was experiencing fit into what I believed was normal. It wasn't. Abuse is not normal or acceptable. I was young and naive, and hindsight is twenty-twenty.

While your normal may be different from mine, there's one thing

Since abusers don't have strength and goodness, they look for women who possess those qualities and then use those traits for themselves.

we have in common: our abusers didn't choose us because we were broken, but because of the amazing women we are. Since abusers don't have strength and goodness, they look for women who possess those qualities and then use those traits for themselves. An abuser can pretend to be a fairy tale prince long enough to entrap the best of us, even if you grew up in a great family. And before long, we begin to see the world through his twisted sense of normal . . . until we wake up one day and see it for what it really is.

ABUSE SNEAKS UP ON YOU

What does abuse look like? It's not taught in school or church. It catches you by surprise. You might think it's an anomaly until it happens again. You blame his job, all the pressure he's under, and coworkers who don't appreciate him. Eventually, he makes sure you know *you're* the problem. You *make* him this way. If only you didn't _____ (fill in the blank) then he wouldn't _____ (fill in the blank).

It's no wonder we're confused and frightened. We've been trained to believe our abuser loves us and our abusive lives are normal. To be sure we are all on the same page, let's be perfectly clear about what domestic abuse is. Experts tells us that naming our fears, naming our emotions, and naming what happened to us is key to recovery. So let's find names for the nightmares we experienced.

There are two types of domestic violence/abuse, also called intimate partner abuse: situational couple violence (SCV) and coercive controlling violence (CCV),[5] also called intimate terrorism. According to WebMD, 86 percent of all reported cases of domestic abuse are coercive control and only 14 percent are considered to be battered women's syndrome or situational couple violence.

Because the battered spouse has obvious injuries, situational couple violence is relatively easy to identify. However, coercive control is a bit harder to recognize, so let's dig into what it looks like a little more.

PHYSICAL VIOLENCE SEXUAL

POWER AND CONTROL

USING COERCION AND THREATS
Making and/or carrying out threats to do something to hurt her • threatening to leave her, to commit suicide, to report her to welfare • making her drop charges • making her do illegal things.

USING INTIMIDATION
Making her afraid by using looks, actions, gestures • smashing things • destroying her property • abusing pets • displaying weapons.

USING ECONOMIC ABUSE
Preventing her from getting or keeping a job • making her ask for money • giving her an allowance • taking her money • not letting her know about or have access to family income.

USING EMOTIONAL ABUSE
Putting her down • making her feel bad about herself • calling her names • making her think she's crazy • playing mind games • humiliating her • making her feel guilty.

USING MALE PRIVILEGE
Treating her like a servant • making all the big decisions • acting like the "master of the castle" • being the one to define men's and women's roles

USING ISOLATION
Controlling what she does, who she sees and talks to, what she reads, where she goes • limiting her outside involvement • using jealousy to justify actions.

USING CHILDREN
Making her feel guilty about the children • using the children to relay messages • using visitation to harass her • threatening to take the children away.

MINIMIZING, DENYING AND BLAMING
Making light of the abuse and not taking her concerns about it seriously • saying the abuse didn't happen • shifting responsibility for abusive behavior • saying she caused it.

PHYSICAL VIOLENCE SEXUAL

www.TheDuluthModel.org

POWER AND CONTROL WHEEL[6]

- Using Coercion and Threats: This can look like the abuser putting you in impossible situations, so that no matter what you choose you will be wrong. He may use physical abuse or the promise of physical abuse to get the response he wants from you, which gives him all the power and you none.
- Using Intimidation: With a look, maybe even a word or a slight movement, he can send shivers up your spine. You know what is coming next if you don't stop or start doing what he wants.

When he does show anger, he destroys your possessions or throws them away, then acts as though it was an accident. I know things are just things, that we can't take them with us when we die, but that knowledge doesn't take away the loss we experience when our things are destroyed.

- Using Emotional Abuse: Emotional abuse includes verbal abuse which, by design, is meant to tear away at your identity. He uses words to lambaste, slash, berate, denounce, vilify, attack, chastise, flay, condemn, and revile you. He'll gaslight you by getting you to believe what is real isn't, designed to make you look crazy and unbalanced until you no longer know what to believe.

- Using Isolation: The goal is to separate you from those who love you, including God. You are the abuser's possession, you belong to him and no one else. He may control what you wear, what you weigh, how you fold the towels or organize your kitchen. He may control what you eat and when you eat, whether you drive a car or walk. He may take pleasure that other men look at you, then blame you for enticing them.

- Minimizing, Denying, and Blaming: If he hurts you physically (not necessarily beating you up—it could be a pinch, a punch, a twist, a pull, a yank) and you react in pain, he'll tell you it wasn't that bad, that you should stop crying or acting like a baby. He'll disregard your emotions and pain as trivial or as overreacting or blame you by saying, If you didn't pull away you wouldn't have been hurt. Saying it's all your fault because you did _____, so he did _____. It's never his fault or as bad as you think it is.

- Using Children: If you show your children too much affection, he may get jealous and demand your attention, or he may punish the kids. If you're in a custody battle, he'll use your kids as a weapon to control you and get what he wants from you. He may even turn your kids against you.

- Using Male Privilege: He twists the stories about patriarchy in the Bible to defend a belief that women are lesser than men. Since he considers himself superior, what he says goes, your opinion doesn't matter, and your value only comes as you serve him and meet his needs.

- Using Ecomomic Abuse: He may keep you in debt, hide money from you, take you off the checking account or health insurance. He may want you to quit your job to take care of the kids, or he may demand that you get a job so you can't take care of your kids. If you get an inheritance, he may take it. What is yours becomes his, and what is his is not yours. He may have the latest vehicle, gadgets, and clothes, while you and the kids may shop at second-hand stores and drive an old car.

The abuser uses violent and nonviolent tactics to strip you of your identity, your will, and your voice. Because the abuse happens over time and sometimes in small ways, you can't always see it for what it is. It's difficult to put into words, to define what he does to you.

For thirty years I lived in oblivion, thinking this was my lot in life, only to discover there are names and definitions for what I experienced. Add *narcissist* to all the above and you get *A Nightmare on Elm Street* instead of *Happily Ever After*. Can you identify?

People who haven't been where we are don't understand why we put up with all this and more. The conditioning we experienced kept us focused on him and his pain and on the extraordinary fear of consequences should we challenge him.

Admitting that none of your marriage was real, that you held no value to him is beyond hard; it's also a defining moment, a moment that makes us wonder why we're still here. Most of us experience this point during the marriage. Admitting we're abused means admitting we're a victim, and none of us want to be a victim. Yet, it's in that "stick a fork in me, I'm done" moment when we wake up from the nightmare and can begin to create a new ending.

It can feel overwhelming, it can feel as though a stranger is the proverbial fly on the wall in your own home . . . seeing the secrets hidden behind closed doors. Take a deep breath, slowly release. You are strong enough to find real healing. As insignificant as that breath seemed, scientists have proven it can ease the tension. So take that deep, cleansing breath anytime you need it.

A NEW LIFE

I settled into life in Texas, bouncing back and forth from my sister's home to my brother's home until March, when my mom helped me get into an apartment. I had twenty-seven days to settle in before I began my new career in corporate America. I was fifty-one, living on my own for the first time in my life. It was sweet and scary all at the same time.

How do I do life and not implode? I had no bandwidth for this. I'd been in slavery for so long that freedom was scary and enticing as I navigated my new life. I took most of my messiness and locked it in a box to deal with later and pretended to be strong and capable.

It brings a whole new meaning to what Israel experienced when they suddenly found themselves free from slavery. They'd spent generations living under a tyrant who was afraid of losing his slaves. But God brought a rescuer in the unlikely form of Moses, who confronted the Egyptian ruler.

The Israelites saw God show up, even as life became unbearable. Their own fear blinded them to what God was doing on their behalf. They saw him act through ten creepy, disgusting, and horrific plagues, until Pharaoh just wanted them gone.

Thus began their journey into freedom. It was anything but easy. They would have to fight for their freedom and keep fighting for it. At times it was more than they could handle even with the presence of God guiding them. You'd think it would be easy since they could physically see God in the form of a cloud by day and a pillar of fire by night. I don't know about you, but there have been times I wished God would direct me with signals of fire and clouds. But God's clear presence didn't seem to help the Israelites. Human nature being what it is, the Israelites still doubted God when he led them to a place where they had seemingly no way out. They were stuck between the approaching Egyptian army bristling with weapons and anger, and a sea they had no way to cross. Maybe you're there yourself—facing poverty, loneliness, raising kids on your own, wondering how you'll balance it all. Some days all you want to do is crawl under the covers and pretend you're anywhere but here.

My guess is that you and I both have thought, like the Israelites did, that God has no idea what he is doing. Then again, God's thoughts are far beyond our own limited thinking. For the Israelites, they didn't know God was going to show off once again, to reveal more of who he is and how much he loved them, even when they fretted, moaned, groaned, and complained.

Did you know that fear of the unknown is what most drives women to go back to their abusers?

They wondered what God was doing and in a moment of panic decided it would be better to go back to their abusers than to risk the unknown.

Did you know that fear of the unknown is what most drives women to go back to their abusers? With our abuser we know what to expect. Fear of the future is so much more terrifying.

The Israelite people romanticized their life in Egypt, blaming Moses for making them leave. Even though they begged God to free them, when he did, they blamed him for how hard it was: an army on one side, the sea on the other. Better alive in bondage than dead in the desert.

Yet just as God had their backs, he has yours. The angel of the Lord and the cloud of God's presence stood between the Israelites and Egypt. When fear rears its ugly head to blind you and distort your thinking, remember that what God did for Israel, he will do for you. God told Israel to get moving as Moses lifted his staff and the winds blew. Can you imagine the sight, as the water parted, the soggy sea bottom dried up, and the liberated slaves walked toward their next phase of freedom? And when they watched God unleash his power against the Egyptians, they were filled with awe and put their faith in him.

Through the centuries God would remind Israel that he was the one who rescued them. When their faith failed, he wanted them to remember what he had already done for them. Why was this so important for Israel to remember? Because at times throughout their history, life would become overwhelming as Israel faced enemies too powerful to conquer. They needed to remember that if God did it for them once, he would do it again. And again. And again.

This story is repeated throughout Scripture as a reminder for us

> God tells us not to be shocked or afraid, that he goes ahead of us, will fight for us, and cares for us as a father cares for his children.

too. It's a beautiful picture of God's protection and the lengths he will go to for his children. His promises aren't just for Israel. In Deuteronomy 1:29–31, God tells us not to be shocked or afraid, that he goes ahead of us, will fight for us, and cares for us as a father cares for his children. You, BeLoved, are his child.

Now that you are free from your abuser, are you ready to start your freedom journey? In moments when you feel like you can't move forward, you'll want to remember why you left. It will become difficult, and at times you'll want to quit and just stay where you are or even think of going back. But I encourage you to keep moving. Remember the name you've given your nightmare and refuse to go back to that nightmarish version of "normal."

If you are still in your marriage, you may be wavering about what to do next—to stay or go. This, dear one, is a decision only you can make. If you decide to go, plan and be safe.

BeLoved, life awaits on the other side. God wants to change the nightmare into a beautiful dream you won't want to wake up from. No longer a victim but a survivor.

"How precious are your thoughts about me, O God. They cannot be numbered! I can't even count them; they outnumber the grains of sand! And when I wake up, you are still with me!" (Psalm 139:17–18).

ENCOUNTER GOD

You are my precious daughter, I am your bodyguard, I will lead you to safety, and heal your broken heart. I fill you with goodness, satisfy your thirst for more of me. You are my masterpiece, my symphony, my poem, and the apple of my eye.

-Your Abba Father
(Psalm 145:20; 107:7, 9; Ephesians 2:10;
Zephaniah 3:17; Mark 14:36)

REACHING FOR MORE

You may or may not be into fairy tales, yet when you met him you may have started to believe that fairy tales really do come true when you find someone you love, who loves you in return. But there was a moment when you became unenchanted, waking up not in a dream but in a nightmare.

1. Were you looking for the fairy tale or did it find you?
2. What have you learned about domestic abuse?
3. What was normal for you prior to meeting your husband?
4. Create a list of any incidents you remember when your husband mistreated you in your marriage. The purpose of the list is to remind you of what he did, no matter how insignificant it may seem. You may have days when you'll waver or think it wasn't that bad, and this will serve as an important reminder. It's also a record that you may need to show your attorney.
5. Reread the story of Abigail (1 Samuel 25) and Israel (Exodus 14:15–31). Can you catch a glimmer of hope? If so, what does hope look like for you? If not, ask Jesus to give you a glimpse.

PART 2

SURVIVOR

Learning to Breathe Again

Are you tired of wallowing in the pit your ex-husband created for you? As long as he can keep you in the pit, he can continue controlling you even if you're no longer with him. Yet there is more to this life than living in constant pain.

Moving forward isn't just about you. It's about the legacy you leave behind for future generations. Today you can change the legacy you leave your family and friends. When you begin healing, you can help walk others through their pain. It is your past, but it's their present. This is especially important if you have children.

Let's look at how not just to survive, but to live. Remember, you're not alone, and God will never ask you to do something without his presence.

"And I am certain that God, who began the good work within you, will continue his work until it is finally finished on the day Christ Jesus returns" (Philippians 1:6).

CHAPTER 4

UNSTUCK

*When the Anguish in Your Soul
Longs to Be Released*

*I hear the Lord saying, "I will stay close to you, instructing
and guiding you along the pathway for your life. I will
advise you along the way and lead you forth with my eyes
as your guide. So don't make it difficult; don't be stubborn
when I take you where you've not been before. Don't make
me tug you and pull you along. Just come with me!"*
—Psalm 32:8–9 (TPT)

In the midst of my healing, I longed for release, yet felt trapped on a roller coaster of pain and grief with stretches of hope. There were days I was sure that if I'd made a different choice, there would have been a different outcome of my circumstances. No matter what I did, I couldn't change the outcome. How about you?

Can you feel the excruciating pain pulverizing your body, soul, and spirit? The abuser made you the villain while he acted like the hero. Maybe you left him, which exposed him, and since he couldn't hide any longer, he went into damage control by spreading lies about you until you looked like the crazy one. Or maybe you're still with him, and you are feeling trapped on your own roller-coaster ride.

Overwhelmed with wave after wave of pain, just when you catch your breath you're sucked under again. You may still be reeling from the shock of all he did to you and your kids, yet to the public, he has it all together and you're the one losing your mind. All you want is your life back, but you're terrified of him. Flipping through family photos, you see how happy you all seemed, yet deep in your soul, you know life behind closed doors was anything but happy and idyllic.

That's when you begin asking *why*. Why did God allow the abuse? Why didn't he intervene? Why didn't God change him? Why does no one see my abuser's cruelty? Why am I the liar? Why didn't he love me? Why wasn't I enough for him? Why is he the one everyone believes? Isn't God in control? If he is, then he doesn't care about me—God must see me as the guilty one. I'm the one paying the price for my abuser's behavior, so I must be at fault.

By the end of my marriage I believed God was impotent and cared for others more than he cared for me. I felt like a five-year-old asking God question after question. Where were you? How come you didn't stop the abuse? *Why? Why? Why?* When no answer came, I concluded I must have done something wrong which is why God punished me and not Guy.

It's normal to get stuck in the repetition of *why* questions. It's part of the process of grieving and healing. God created you to be curious, to wonder, to discover. It's no surprise that, out of our trauma, we wonder where God was and why he didn't stop the abuse or cause our abuser to repent and change his ways.

God can feel far away, especially if you feel your prayers and cries are bouncing off the ceiling. I understand if all you want are answers, and all you seem to get is deafening silence. When you demand to know *why*, you're asking God to explain himself.

Dear one, the answers to our questions are facts and don't ease the pain. They may sink us even deeper into more pain, since the answers sound like excuses for our abuser's behavior.

For example, the answer can consist of a textbook description of a narcissist, or an explanation of the habits or lifestyle of an addict. The answer tends to make you believe there is a reason—and therefore an excuse—for the abuser's actions. The facts don't help you heal; they often cause more pain and condemnation.

Asking why leads into "if only . . ."

If only I was a better wife.

If only I'd been a better mom.

If only I didn't leave him.

If only I'd left sooner.

If only I'd told my family.

If only leads to a path of regret, in which you are convinced if you had made another choice the outcome would be different. No matter what you did differently, the result would be the same. In your abuser's eyes, he can't be at fault, so the fault must be yours.

You may have stayed in the abuse for a few months or several years until you couldn't take it anymore and fled. Or maybe divorce was thrust on you, and it wasn't what you wanted. You want the dream back, but it's like squeezing toothpaste out of a tube—you can't put it back once it's out.

HOPING FOR THE BEST

Until June 2004, I prayed and hoped Guy would become a better man. I lived for the good times, dreaded the bad, until three decades of my life was gone. As Christians, we hope for the best, we know nothing is impossible for God. The Bible is full of stories about how God transformed people like the countless women Jesus encountered—the woman at the well, the woman caught in adultery, Mary Magdalene, to name a few—and performed miracles by healing the blind, the deaf, the bent, the broken, and the crippled, and touching the untouchable to heal them of leprosy. We live for miracles of biblical proportion that never seem to happen for us. Then we may wonder what we did to make God angry, which reinforces our belief that something is wrong with us. *If only . . .*

Our view of God gets wrapped up in our view of our husband. We begin to believe our husband is more powerful than God. We may even believe God is blessing him, and you and I are evil because we are losing everything. This is a lie from the father of lies, the rebellious creature we call Satan. Satan once tried to take over from God. He failed miserably. But now Satan's number one desire is to hit God where it hurts most. And since God loves you and me more than anything, Satan will do anything to separate us from God. He twists truth and makes it look like God is behind our abuse when it is entirely our abuser's responsibility. This liar takes the beauty of love and partnership and distorts it into pain and bondage. Not only does the enemy lie to us, so do our husbands when they covertly blame us for their behavior. There may be a part of us that thinks, if only we could do something different life would change, our husbands would change. When it doesn't we may begin to believe we are the problem.

You may be angry at God, which is understandable. The Psalms are full of David's whys. Why would King Saul, who said he loved David, turn on David in jealous rages? At times David was angry and in deep anguish, wondered where God was. Although David had been anointed as king, he was hunted by King Saul, who wanted to kill David. Like you and I, David struggled with God's seeming lack of action.

In Psalm 10:1, David prayed, "O Lord, why do you stand so far away? Why do you hide when I am in trouble?" Then in verses 2–15, David complained about those who were trying to destroy him and wondered what God would do about it. Isn't it comforting to know that David, the one God calls a man after his own heart, was confused and frustrated with God? Isn't it freeing to know we can call out to God and ask questions?

However, by verses 16–18, David declared, "The Lord is king." Do you find that as interesting as I do? David is in anguish and somehow finds a way to trust. And this reversal isn't the only time David finds his way back to God.

Psalm 13 reveals David's roller coaster of emotions ranging from sorrow, anger, and rage, to trust and praise, all within a few sentences:

> O Lord, how long will you forget me? Forever?
>   How long will you look the other way?
> How long must I struggle with anguish in my soul,
>   with sorrow in my heart every day?
>   How long will my enemy have the upper hand?
>
> Turn and answer me, O Lord my God!
>   Restore the sparkle to my eyes, or I will die.

Don't let my enemies gloat, saying, "We have defeated him!"
    Don't let them rejoice at my downfall.

But I trust in your unfailing love.
    I will rejoice because you have rescued me.
I will sing to the LORD
    because He is good to me.

Part of the key to surviving is coming back to the promises of God, even though you don't understand all the whys of what happened to you. If you don't find your way back to God, this place of misery can send you over the edge into despair and deception. That doesn't mean this return to God's promises happens quickly or easily. Your tears and frustration may last a while. That's okay. But the fact is that Satan steals from you and attempts to destroy and ultimately kill you emotionally and/or physically.

Here's something you need to know: Satan doesn't win.

Here's something you need to know: Satan doesn't win. No matter what it looks like, he hasn't won then, isn't winning now, and won't win in the end.

Evil and good collided the day Jesus hung on the cross surrounded by the hordes of hell hurling insults at him. The moment Jesus breathed his last breath, their mocking shouts ascended into heaven. Their mission was accomplished: The God-man was dead! They defeated the deliverer, the hope of mankind. Lucifer, sitting in the courtroom of heaven, smug with victory, relished the moment he thought he defeated the Great I AM and could take his place on the throne. But it was just that—a moment.

Suddenly, shouts of agony and rage ripped through the universe as Jesus descended into hades to take back what and who was his. "Death is swallowed up in victory. O death, where is your victory? O death where is your sting?" (1 Corinthians 15:54–55).

Jesus struck a blow that day. As a result, we no longer have to walk around as the living dead. Genesis 3:15 was fulfilled, Satan was defeated; he is still defeated. The fallen one acts like a lion; he's a counterfeit. The father of lies wants to keep you from freedom, from knowing your identity in Christ, from walking healed and whole. You can let him have his way—dead to life—or you can choose life in abundance.

For several years, I walked around as the "living dead," pretending I was fine until I couldn't hold up the lie anymore. I was always waiting for the other shoe to drop, because when life was good it was bound to get bad. I didn't realize how much God desired my wholeness. God promises to put our shattered bones back together and put muscle, tendons, and skin on the skeleton, then breathe life into us. Doesn't that sound amazing?

Ezekiel 37 is an extraordinary story of life and death. The Lord took the prophet Ezekiel on a journey to change how he saw and perceived life. The Lord whisked Ezekiel around a valley of dried-up old bones, then asked Ezekiel if he saw life. It's clear from Scripture that Ezekiel only saw death. The Lord told Ezekiel to speak life to the bones. That is part of God's process in your healing. He'll put you back together and breathe life back into you through his Word, encouragement from others, and the sweetness of the Holy Spirit. In the moments when it seems you're stuck in the muck of hopelessness, he'll throw you a lifeline to pull you out.

Where Satan's goal is the destruction of God's BeLoved, God's goal is to heal the brokenhearted. You may feel like you are a dry husk of what you once were. But that isn't freedom. God wants more for you. In fact, he wants to give you more than you can hope or imagine (Ephesians 3:20). He wants you to live in abundance, freedom, and wholeness. What the father of lies twisted for evil, God will use to redeem you when you surrender to him.

Surrender sounds scary after living in abuse. It feels like we're giving up our power after we've worked hard to regain it. Our husbands used surrender to control us, to keep us under their thumbs, to take from us. That isn't who God is. When he asks us to surrender, he's asking us to relinquish the pain and hurt to him, not to control us but to release us from the pit we've been stuck in, so he can give us abundantly more than we can ask or imagine (Ephesians 3:20).

Surrender isn't one and done. It's moment by moment and day by day. The reward of yielding is for our benefit and looks like courage and strength to heal.

GOD ISN'T AFRAID OF OUR UGLY

There will be a day when you may feel fine . . . until you don't. Grief will roll over you like an angry ocean—grief over what you lost and what you never had. Then you'll suck it up, put on your big-girl pants, and move forward . . . until you can't. Hear me when I say, this is normal. It's like when your leg has fallen asleep and suddenly the blood flow is let back in. It tingles and hurts until it wakes up and returns to normal.

This is what we do in the aftermath of abuse. We exist until God breathes life back into us. It will happen. How long it lasts depends on our capacity for healing. God allows you to heal at your own pace. There will be days you don't want to face the pain, and that's okay.

> There will be days you don't want to face the pain, and that's okay.

For myself, I carried too many boxes stuffed with pain. God, in his kindness and mercy, freed me from one box at a time until I was strong enough to face more.

What does it feel like when we're brokenhearted? It may feel bone shattering, like a dull ache, or jagged, intense, crushing, and relentless. Is it any wonder we want the pain to stop? You can almost feel the depth of David's agony when he sang:

> For when the cords of death wrapped around me
> and torrents of destruction overwhelmed me,
> taking me to death's door,
> in my distress I cried out to you, the delivering God,
> and from your temple-throne you heard my troubled cry,
> and my sobs went right into your heart.
> (Psalm 18:4–6 TPT)

You can stay stuck in the agony, remain a victim, or choose to survive. Choose to call out to God, even though you're not sure you trust him yet. He hears your cry, even when you don't have words for your pain. Romans 8:26–27 is a perfect reminder: "But the Holy Spirit prays for us with groanings that cannot be expressed in words. And the Father who knows all hearts knows what the Spirit is saying, for the Spirit pleads for us believers." When we don't know how to pray, the Holy Spirit prays for us with groanings that are too deep for words. Let the Spirit pray for you when you can't put words to your pain and grief.

Jesus isn't afraid of our ugly situation. He consistently wrapped his arms around the broken—touching lepers, healing the bleeding, feeding the hungry. He put hands and feet to the words of his Father: "The LORD is close to the brokenhearted; he rescues those whose spirits are crushed" (Psalm 34:18), and "He heals the brokenhearted and bandages their wounds" (Psalm 147:3).

Jesus is the fulfillment of all the promises of God. Jesus was compassionate toward people, whether they were sick, blind, deaf, possessed, lepers, or broken by life and stuck in the muck of pain. Even though Jesus can't physically touch you, he is compassionate toward you and can still touch you in ways beyond the physical. He can and will heal every part of you. Jesus never promised an easy life; he does promise to heal the abused.

Our heart is our center. The Hebrew word for *heart* refers not to an organ beating in our chest but to our feelings, will, intellect, consent, courage, kindness, understanding, and wisdom. When you are abused, the center of who you are has been crushed into pieces which can paralyze you, leaving you feeling stuck and unable to move forward.

I realize the thought of moving forward at this point may be daunting. Perhaps you feel your dreams are haunted by your *if onlys*. I know what it's like to feel your days are filled with regret for all that's been lost and for all the broken dreams. God invites you to wholeness. Jesus didn't come to save you from your sins just so you'll go to heaven one day. He came to set you free and make you whole. God's promise for salvation isn't limited to the future; salvation is for the here and now. Paul said in Ephesians 3:19, "May you experience the love of Christ, though it is too great to understand fully. Then you will be made complete with all the fullness of life and power that comes from God."

Maybe you can't imagine God's heart is for you. You might be angry at him for not intervening, for not being there, for abandoning you. He's God, all knowing, everywhere all at once. Nothing is impossible for him, so why couldn't he rescue you?

There comes a point when you choose to give up knowing all the whys and why nots. God had one question for me: *Will you trust me?* I'd say yes, then stop to acknowledge I wasn't sure I did trust him. Yet he proved himself faithful.

He may be asking you the same question—*Will you trust me?* He delights in hearing your response even when the answer is, "I'm not sure."

GOD IS GOOD ALL THE TIME

I hope you know how courageous you are. You may not see your bravery, but I do. I know what it took for you to get this far. With each day you grow stronger and break another chain of abuse.

What you lived through can make you stronger, but God doesn't bring tragedy into your life to make you a stronger Christian. Instead, he will use what life hits you with to make you stronger, and he will bring purpose out of your pain. He wastes nothing and uses everything, making sure you're better than before. Romans 8:28 is a familiar verse that reminds us that he causes all things to work together for good. That doesn't mean he brought the bad, but he will use what has happened to us for good. In this moment, that may not sound comforting, it may even sound scary, but one day you'll see what you can't see now.

A friend told me that what I lived through made me the woman I am today. On one level I agree, yet if I had chosen not to marry Guy and had gone into the mission field instead, I would still be the woman I am today but with a different story.

I didn't want to be known as the abused woman. I hated the thought of people looking at me as if I was defective for staying in an abusive marriage for thirty years. I didn't feel brave. I felt like a coward, too afraid to leave, too afraid to trust God to be more powerful than Guy.

I don't know when I chose to survive, to live in spite of the trauma I endured. After I began my new career a few months after I left Guy, I put on a brave front, pretending I was stronger than I was. I held on to the hope that there had to be more to life than what I was living. Though the future held the unknown, I chose to step into it. Going back wasn't an option.

Remember talking about the Israelites when they stood with their backs against the sea and watched as the Egyptian army bore down on them? God told Moses to stand and watch. Then he told the people to move as Moses raised his staff and the Red Sea parted. God's part was to open the sea, Israel's part was to move. You can't do his part, and he won't do yours. (You'll hear me say this a lot.)

Abuse has twisted every area of your life, especially your perception of love and your belief in God's goodness.

I realize I'm asking a lot from you. I'm asking you to step from the known to the unknown, to live until you're alive. I know thinking about it can be paralyzing as the fear seeps into every pore of your body.

Take a deep breath. Breathe out slow. You can do this.

One of the key components of this book is seeing how abuse has twisted every area of your life, especially your perception of love and your belief in God's goodness. You'll find as you read that God is shifting your view of both, to not just *tell* you what love and goodness are, but to *show* you as you heal.

The Song of Songs in the Bible is a love story, but not just between a man and a woman. It's the story of Jesus the Bridegroom and his bride. You, dear one, are his bride, if you are trusting in Jesus alone for your salvation. His love for you is endless and relentless. He won't ask you to do anything that he won't do with you. Are you ready to begin healing?

You must catch the troubling foxes,
    those sly little foxes that hinder our relationship.

For they raid our budding vineyard of love
to ruin what I've planted within you.
Will you catch them and remove them for me?
We will do it together. (Song of Songs 2:15 TPT)

Do you hear your Bridegroom's invitation to healing? The little foxes represent the lies your abuser and the enemy spoke about you and to you. Dear reader, ask Jesus what your little foxes are so you can release them with his help. Then you will discover just how deep his love and goodness for you is.

FIND YOUR SECRET PLACE

The 1987 version of *The Secret Garden* is one of my favorite movies, though I've seen all the film adaptations of the book written by Frances Hodgson Burnett. Mary experiences the tremendous loss of her parents, her home, and what little affection her parents gave her. She travels from India to England, where she stays with a distant relative who becomes her guardian. One day she discovers a wall covered in vines, and believes if there is a wall, there must be a door. She eventually discovers the entry to an overgrown garden. The garden looks lifeless, yet as Mary, Dickon, and Colin pull up the weeds, cut off the dead plants, and till the soil, they find life hidden beneath. In the end, the garden becomes their refuge where Colin learns to walk, where friendship is formed, and where healing takes place.

In Psalm 91:1, we are invited into God's secret garden: "Those who live in the shelter [secret place] of the Most High will find rest in the shadow [protection and refreshment] of the Almighty."

Before we move to the next chapter, won't you join me in an encounter with Jesus? Even when he seems far away, he's walking with you, inviting you out of the muck of abuse and into his secret garden of healing. You can know about him without ever experiencing him. To experience Jesus, engage your imagination and creativity and step into relationship with him.

My secret place is always at the shore, sitting with Jesus on a beach towel, wiggling our toes in the sand. I can hear the roar of the waves, smell the salt in the air, feel the warmth of the sun and the sand between my toes. I feel his strength just being shoulder to shoulder with him, sitting in silence, and enjoying his presence. Now when I picture Jesus, we are still on the beach, standing forehead to forehead, dancing. I feel his love for me, I'm protected, safe in his arms.

Now it's your turn. Ask Jesus to take you to your secret place in your mind where you feel safe. Take your time to *see* where you are, *hear* the sounds around you, *smell* the fragrance in the air, *feel* the breeze or the sun on your skin, engage your *touch*. Invite Jesus to join you. He is already there, but our perception can make us believe he isn't. Talk with him, ask him questions. Feel his heartbeat, look into his eyes, touch him, breathe in the fragrance of him, hear his words. Stay there as long as you want and go back anytime. When you're done, try writing about your experience in a journal. Better yet, write what you're feeling and experiencing while you're still in that moment with him.

ENCOUNTER GOD

My BeLoved, I sent my Son to be your light, hope, and salvation. Jesus is a perfect picture of me. We will lead you from the depths of darkness and gloom threatening to entrap you. Cry out to me, and I will save you from distress. With Jesus you can face the anguish in your soul.

~El Roi—the God who sees
(John 1:5; Matthew 12:21; 2 Corinthians 5:21; John 14:9;
Psalm 107:10, 14, 19; Philippians 4:13; Genesis 16:13)

REACHING FOR MORE

It can be easy to get stuck in the *why*s and *if only*s. You may think the answers to why will bring you solace. They don't. The answers are facts that bring their own pain. Can you consider that there isn't anything you could have done differently to change the outcome once you said "I do"? Are you ready to get unstuck?

1. List out your why questions, then reframe why with *what* or *how* questions to Jesus and write out his response.
2. List out what you think you could have done differently. Then ask Jesus about each one and write out his response.
3. Where do you feel stuck? If there is more than one area, pick one. Write out what action you can do to get unstuck.
4. What does it look like for you to turn to God?
5. You may struggle to trust God. Is there one area where you could take a tiny step toward him? Write out what that looks like.

CHAPTER 5

UNCOVERED

When Facing Pain Is the Only Option

*Mostly what God does is love you. Keep company with him
and learn a life of love. Observe how Christ loved us. His
love was not cautious but extravagant. He didn't love in
order to get something from us but to give everything of
himself to us. Love like that.*

—Ephesians 5:1–2 (MSG)

For I am the LORD who heals you.

—Exodus 15:26

I hid behind a facade of smoke and mirrors to avoid my pain. Now
you see her—now you don't. I looked like I had it all together. But I
was far from it. My strength was in knowledge. I had the right answer
for everything and could help others, but not myself. The by-product
of hiding my pain was that I became numb. I felt nothing. I was in
the Word, heard God, looked and acted like a normal person . . .
but I felt dead.

None of this stopped God from working in my life. I built walls
that were high and deep to keep out the pain and everyone around
me, even thinking I could keep God out too. You'd think I'd want
to be healed, but I didn't want to feel the pain to get there.

Every negative situation in my life created pain and hurt that
became fertile soil for lies to grow. With every bit of negativity, the
lies of rejection, unworthiness, feeling unloved, or not being enough
grew into weeds and defined who I believed I was. I began thinking
It's just the way I am, which is the biggest lie of all.

I saw God as the one who was waiting for me to mess up—the ultimate ogre in the sky, who watched everything I did or didn't do. With every screwup, he'd put a check by my name. *Oh look, she did it again. Check. Check. Check.*

God had more for me than I could ever imagine, but I was clueless. I thought I was healed. Shame and fear were gone, so I was good, right?

Wrong.

For nine years all my healing was vertical, between God and myself. As long as it stayed between God and myself, I could determine how much healing I needed. When it became difficult, I would stop the process and convince myself I was okay.

How did that work for me?

It worked until it didn't. Sound familiar?

Yet God won't leave us without help. Since he is for you and me, he will bring us to the place we need to be in order to find healing.

My healing shifted when I joined a thirteen-week group in which we walked through our past, met our pain head-on, and asked God the difficult questions about where he was in our abuse and what he wanted to say about what we survived. We poured out our rage on the people who caused the pain, we sought the comfort of God, and by the time we reached the last chapter of the workbook, we chose to forgive those who hurt us. We learned that not only does abuse happen in relationships, but our healing does as well.

> God is gracious, kind, and patient. He doesn't want to retraumatize you.

Healing often happens like this: God peels your pain like an onion. The stronger you get, the more layers he can peel off. You have no choice but to depend on him. If you decide you can't or don't want to do it, no worries. He'll wait for you. Like dirty dishes don't wash themselves, your pain will wait for you. God is gracious, kind, and patient. He doesn't want to retraumatize you.

Are you ready for God to peel back the layers of your life in order to face the trauma and pain? You won't know what to expect or what will be uncovered from the depths of your soul.

When I learned to live again, to put one foot in front of the other, to step out, to begin the process of peeling away the layers of false identity and discover who I was, I was able to shift my source from myself to him. It's a grueling process. It wasn't pretty as I traversed into unknown territory. It's not uncommon to fall back into the pattern of being a victim, to become poor pitiful me again. I'd move five steps forward and fall back seven. When it became more difficult, I'd stop altogether.

Like mine, the abuse you lived under didn't begin overnight and won't heal overnight. Healing takes time, hard work, and trust when you don't understand where God was and why he didn't stop it. You'll wonder why the man who vowed to love you didn't love you enough to be a better man. At some point, that's all you'll want to understand. Prayerfully, you will one day decide to trust God, even though you don't understand. It may seem impossible now, but that day can be today.

Are you willing to take the risk in order to be healed?

THE AGONY

As you choose to face the pain, I want to remind you that God's love is extravagant, limitless, boundless, and exorbitant. Pain will lie and tell you you're unlovable to God, which is far from the truth. In Romans 8:38, Paul reminds us that nothing can separate us from God's love, not even pain or your abuser.

Pain will tell you God is to blame, he could have stopped it, but he did nothing. In your blame, you assign to God the works of the fallen one. When you turn to Jesus, even in the midst of pain, he will remove the veil so you can see clearly how much he loves you and watches over you even in the abuse.

In Ephesians 3:19, Paul wrote, "May you experience the love of Christ, though it is too great to understand fully." The word *experience* in some translations means "to know" or "to perceive."

To perceive is to become aware and recognize what may not be clear or obvious. Abuse can cause you to believe God's love has faded. BeLoved, you can become aware of God's love again. The only way to face the pain is to embrace the love of God. His greatest expression of love is his Son Jesus. "So the Word became human and made his home among us. He was full of unfailing love and faithfulness" (John 1:14).

Jesus is our promise that we will one day be healed. Luke 4:18–19 records that Jesus announced that he came to release the captives, the oppressed, and the blind. The captives are those taken as prisoners by others and held against their will. The oppressed are the broken-hearted. The blind are those who can't see, including those who can't see that they're in pain.

There may be times as you face the pain when you'll wonder if God *does* love you, especially when it seems your abuser isn't suffering any consequences and no one sees who he really is.

Your Abba Father isn't asking you to face anything he won't face with you. When it gets difficult—and I assure you it will—go into your secret place with Jesus. Even as I write, I am praying for you, and it is my hope that you will discover what I did: God *never once* abandoned you. Even though it may feel like he has, he never stopped loving you. The father of lies cannot counterfeit God's love or presence. For me, God's presence is like being covered in warm oil, wrapped in a comfy blanket, and held securely in his lap. You may not be able to imagine living without chaos—that cycle of relief because you're free of your abuser and terror about how you'll live in the future. You may be running for your life, hiding, hoping he doesn't find you. You may wish you could go back, that he would change and life would be perfect again. Then reality hits . . . it was only perfect for him while you and your children suffered in your attempts to appease him.

I know, dear one. The pain rolls in like waves. At first, the waves seem enticing and gentle, growing larger and stronger in intensity until you're consumed. The effects of the abuse you experienced haunt you like a night terror you can't wake up from.

Pain is described as an ache, agony, misery, despondency, an open wound, trauma, or affliction. Pain can be physical, emotional, or both. I define pain as the agony in my soul that destroys my identity, my hope, and my belief that God is good.

Physical pain tells us our bodies have been damaged. Think about that. That means physical pain is a healthy warning sign. Without pain, you and I wouldn't know if we broke a bone or burned our hand. Pain is a warning that something is dreadfully wrong and needs to be fixed. We'll go to the doctor or a hospital to find out what's wrong when we're in physical pain. Yet when we are in *emotional* pain due to abuse, we often bury the pain rather than bring it to light so we can heal from the ache in our souls. But this is exactly where healing begins.

> "Just as damaging as a madman shooting a deadly weapon is someone who lies to a friend and then says, 'I was only joking'" (Proverbs 26:18-19).

FACING THE PAIN OF VERBAL, EMOTIONAL, AND PSYCHOLOGICAL ABUSE

Verbal, emotional, and psychological abuse are the center of coercive control; the effects leave bruises we can't see and destroy the core of who we are. It was the foundation of my relationship with Guy. He would say something to expose my deepest insecurity, followed by the words, "Just joking." Scripture tells us: "Just as damaging as a madman shooting a deadly weapon is someone who lies to a friend and then says, 'I was only joking'" (Proverbs 26:18–19).

A friend of mine once described emotional pain as one of the deepest forms of pain she's ever experienced. It made me physically ill to hear her description of the twisted, degrading things her husband said to her. Emotional pain is soul crushing, life sucking, and hope ravaging. It includes anything from verbal abuse and constant criticism to more subtle tactics, such as intimidation, manipulation, and refusal to ever be pleased.

Psychological abuse includes emotional and verbal abuse. Gaslighting—assigning motives to your actions that aren't your intent—attacks your reality and is designed to make you look crazy to the point that you question everything you know about events you both experienced. He'll change how the event happened, when it happened, what you wore at the time, until you believe you've lost your mind. Narcissistic abusers may even drive you to attempt suicide, and you'll even think it's your idea. It's meant to keep you off balance, so that if you ever reveal what he is truly like, no one would believe you.

The constant attack through words and silence will destroy your self-confidence and control every area of your life . . . how you dress, where you work, who your friends are, what you say. You'll be criticized until you conform to what he deems is the right behavior.

Verbal and emotional abuse are intermixed. One can't operate without the other, and they don't require rage or anger. They are cold and calculating. Verbal abuse is used with pinpoint accuracy to hit the intended target in the most vulnerable places of her body, soul, and spirit.

You'll begin to echo what he speaks about you until you believe what he believes about you. When you look in the mirror you won't see you—you'll see a distorted image of yourself. I'm sure you've heard the old saying, Sticks and stones may break my bones, but words will never hurt me. That is the greatest lie perpetrated throughout our childhood. Negative words destroy who we are until nothing is left of our identity.

Those who downplay the effects of the violence of verbal, emotional, and psychological abuse ignore huge amounts of research and don't understand the damage caused from the constant barrage of punches that leave no physical bruises but wound the soul.

Countless women stay in verbally and emotionally abusive marriages believing they have no grounds to leave. They often wish their husbands would just hit them to stop the bombardment of painful words. Calling the police isn't an option since there aren't any visible injuries. It's the abuser's word against theirs.

Since he's a charmer, he talks himself out of any situation, making sure people know you are the problem, not him. He's calm, while you're frantic with anxiety and fear. Others can't imagine there's a monster lurking beneath his calm demeanor.

I know how unbelievably hard it is to see your marriage played out in a book. You might even wonder if I met you or your husband or if your husband and mine read the same handbook—*How to Abuse Your Family in Ten Easy Steps and Get Away with It.*

Healing from the violence of words takes a long time. Those words replay in your mind, especially in the quiet. You may even find yourself using the same words about yourself when you do something wrong. It's as if they are lodged in your brain. BeLoved, God will replace those words with his words as you read his Word, as you sit in his presence.

FACING THE PAIN OF COERCIVE CONTROL

Your abuser used brutality, cruelty, and dominance to annihilate every part of who you are. He controlled every area of your life, gaslighted you until you doubted your sanity, and with one look, he could send you into chaos and bone-shattering terror. He used every opportunity to take your voice, choice, will, and identity to devalue and depersonalize you.

It's called intimate terrorism for a reason, he used mostly non-violent and maybe some violent tactics to intimidate and force you to do and be who he wanted you to be, the complete, blindly submissive Stepford wife. (*The Stepford Wives* is a book that was adapted into movies in 1975 and 2004.)

He taught you how to respond to him; he isolated you so that he would be your only authority and source of life. He ate away at your beliefs until you believed what he believed, until he became your god. You became addicted to trauma and chaos, and now often wonder why quiet and peace seem foreign. You may even create chaos when life seems peaceful.

You may find yourself jumping at the smallest sound, or you may be startled if someone comes up behind you, sending warnings throughout your body of impending danger. You may question every choice you make and question your sanity on a regular basis.

You were his target and possession to use and abuse. To him it is normal and satisfying.

Facing this pain is just plain hard and takes time. There isn't an easy way through it, you may have PTSD and Complex PTSD. You may need a trauma therapist to help you heal. Don't be afraid to break out of your isolated pattern and reach out for help.

FACING THE PAIN OF PHYSICAL ABUSE

Don't think for one moment that if you weren't physically abused you weren't in an abusive marriage. Many women don't experience physical abuse, or at least don't think they have because their husbands never hit them, or hit them only once.

Physical abuse can be classified as anything from broken bones, black eyes, broken teeth, bruises, strangulation, stabs, starvation, impacts on the head with a firearm (yes, Guy did that once), to being pinched, gripped, poked, squeezed, pulled, or threatened with physical harm through a look or gesture. You may feel pain from old wounds, carry the scars on your body, or shudder in fear if someone looks at you wrong.

The trauma of physical abuse will fade long before the trauma of the other types of abuse. Though physical scars last a lifetime, the scars on your soul will heal as if the wound never existed. You may hold the memories for years, but eventually memories fade into a distant past.

Physical abuse can also look like symptoms and illnesses such as depression, anxiety, chronic fatigue, fibromyalgia, headaches, insomnia, gastrointestinal issues, heart palpitations, panic attacks, autoimmune disorders, endocrine breakdown, unbalanced hormones, and brain fog, to name a few.

He may not have hit you, yet you carry the trauma of his abuse in your body. These physical responses to abuse can stay with you for the remainder of your life. Some may ease or disappear as you heal.

FACING THE PAIN OF SPIRITUAL ABUSE

Out of all the trauma you face, spiritual abuse may be the most difficult since you are retraumatized due to bad advice from church leadership or from those who think they are offering biblical advice on marriage.

When you choose to leave your abuser, you may be ostracized by the church for seeking divorce. Some women have been told they are going to hell if they get a divorce, even though he is an abuser and doesn't treat his wife as a man should.

You may lose friends who may side with him, since after all, he is sorry or has spun a tale of woe for having put up with your unbalanced behavior. Friends may also disappear if the church sides with him because the leadership or members don't believe you.

> Your view of God can be warped by your abuser because he placed himself as God in your life.

Your view of God can be warped by your abuser because he placed himself as God in your life. That makes it difficult to separate the two. Your anger is also focused on God because surely he could or should have stopped your husband.

This pain is difficult to face due to the betrayal and rejection from fellow believers. It's not unusual for women to leave the church after the treatment they have received from the bride of Christ. While the church is supposed to be the earthly representatives of God, they often get it so very, very wrong.

How do you face this pain? You recall the character of God—good, love, peace, and so on—and separate him from the character of your abuser. Search the Scriptures, specifically the Psalms, where David often cried out to God, wondering if God saw his pain or his enemies and why he didn't stop evil. David's words sound as if he was accusing God, but in the end he acknowledges who God is and praises him for his goodness and protection.

It may sound counterintuitive to praise when you're in pain, when you're not even sure you trust God. But it's not. It's an act of faith when your faith may be wavering.

Let the cry of your heart be Psalm 55. Here are a few choice nuggets from its verses:

Verse 1: "Listen to my prayer, O God. Do not ignore my cry for help!"

Verses 4–5: "My heart pounds in my chest. The terror of death assaults me. Fear and trembling overwhelm me, and I can't stop shaking."

Verses 12–14: "It is not an enemy who taunts me—I could bear that. It is not my foes who so arrogantly insult me—I could have hidden from them. Instead, it is you—my equal, my companion and close friend. What good fellowship we once enjoyed as we walked together to the house of God."

Verse 16: "I will call on God, and the LORD will rescue me."

Verses 20–22: "As for my companion, he betrayed his friends; he broke his promises. His words are as smooth as butter, but in his heart is war. His words are as soothing as lotion, but underneath are daggers! Give your burdens to the LORD, and he will take care of you. He will not permit the godly to slip and fall."

When it may feel as though God has abandoned you and is blessing your ex-husband because you are experiencing his consequences while he seems to get off scot-free, you can know God does not, will not, and cannot bless abuse. You look beyond what your eyes see and know that God will not violate his character.

The enemy, though, has no problem mimicking God, to trick us into thinking God isn't who he says he is. God can handle your anger, and he is patient and kind in the process.

FACING THE PAIN OF SEXUAL ABUSE

I thought sex was the part of my previous marriage that was normal. Even after I got out and remarried, I struggled to identify the emotions I felt about Guy and my sex life . . . until it all came back to me in a dream.

Tears, anxiety, and arousal aren't my normal for four in the morning. The dream didn't feel like a dream—it felt real. I experienced disgust, revulsion, and repulsion. As I woke sobbing, I didn't know who I was in bed with. It felt as if I'd been transported back to my time with Guy. My only desire was to touch my sweet husband, Tom, to remind me of my present and to wipe the nightmare from my mind and emotions, but fear intervened.

In the dream I felt used and abused as Guy manipulated my body to respond. He made me think it was all about me. Now I realize it was just another way he controlled and manipulated me. Saying no to him wasn't an option. Punishment, rejection, and silence would ensue. After the silence, rage would explode, then the demand for sex to appease him.

To him, I was rejecting him if I didn't want to be touched, especially in front of our children. Let's face it. How many women like to be touched when PMS is raging? Much less be groped. It was a rule that only he was allowed to say, "Not tonight, honey." I had no right to refuse.

I didn't understand why I felt used, dirty, and manipulated. I couldn't explain how I felt at the time. Twelve years later, the dream uncovered the truth of how I felt but could never describe.

Looking back, I can see how his needs became my own. It made me sick to realize how he manipulated sex throughout our marriage. Sex was always about Guy, even my pleasure was about him, since he controlled what I did or didn't experience. Some abusers will call you horrible, humiliating names to make you feel dirty; they will even ask you to do things that will cause you to feel degraded—including inviting porn in—and you begin to think it's all normal and all your idea.

You may believe you hated sex. What if what you hated was how your abuser made you feel rather than the act itself? It's difficult to be in the mood when he's called you degrading names throughout the day until you would feel as if you are less than nothing.

Sexual abuse isn't just the act. It's what happens before and after. It's also the way he talks about your body, touching you in front of the kids, sharing intimate details in front of the kids or with other people. He may introduce you to porn, he may even compare you to who he sees on the screen—"Why can't you look like her and do what she does?"

He may have betrayed you by cheating on you. He may have given you sexually transmitted diseases and blamed his cheating on something you did or did not do.

TIME TO TAKE A DEEP BREATH

I imagine by now you might be feeling an abundance of emotions. Take a deep breath . . . now let it out. Do you need to set the book down? Maybe you want to scream at the top of your lungs at the rush of memories and emotions rolling over you. The way you're feeling now is the result of being emotionally triggered. I define being triggered as having long-buried emotions flood to the surface when you are retraumatized from a similar event. You'll be thrust into a whirlwind of panic and pain, leaving you a puddle on the floor.

Pain is a lousy decision maker. You and I do everything conceivable to avoid pain. We numb it, medicate it, deny it, cover it up, or dress it up. To the world we look fine. The pain we are trying to avoid is still pain, we just tend to call it by a different name. You may think pain is the issue. The pain is only the symptom that tells you there's a deeper problem. In time, the pain becomes a land mine. When someone steps on your land mine, the mine blows up and everyone around you is wounded. Sometimes you'll step on your own land mine to avoid feeling the pain.

> Facing the pain will take every ounce of courage you have; it's risky and takes audacity and boldness to keep moving forward.

My pain would become unbearable in the quiet of the mornings and at night as I fell asleep. During the week, I was able to keep from dealing with the pain by working. On the weekends, shopping, soaking up the sun, and going to church kept me from dealing with pain. Distraction worked for me for thirty years, so I figured it would work for a lifetime. Think about it for a moment. How do *you* deal with *your* pain?

Facing the pain will take every ounce of courage you have; it's risky and takes audacity and boldness to keep moving forward. You may think you don't have what it takes, but remember you aren't alone. Jesus is with you in the pain.

The woman in Mark 5:25–34 had been bleeding for twelve years. She spent all her money on doctors who weren't able to cure her, but made her condition worse. She was considered "unclean," according to Jewish law, which meant no one could touch her or they would be considered unclean too. She did all she could to be healed, spending the only money she had on whatever doctor or treatment might cure her. Yet nothing worked, and now she was broke. She was desperate enough to risk her life in order to find relief. She heard about Jesus, the man who healed the sick and opened blind eyes. Certainly he could heal her if everything she heard about him was true. If she could only *touch* him. Inching her way through the crowd, she reached out to touch Jesus.

The moment she touched him she felt healing flow through her body as she slipped into the crowd. Jesus felt the power leave his body. He asked, "Who touched me?" His disciples thought he was out of his mind, asking such a question. Yet by asking, he was inviting her to risk even more by telling her story. I imagine Jesus looking straight at her as he asked the question. Scripture says she fell at his feet, telling her story to all who could hear. When she finished, Jesus said, "Daughter, you took a risk of faith, and now you're healed and whole. Live well, live blessed!" (MSG).

This woman had been an outcast for twelve long years. She was desperate and in need of help. By touching Jesus, she risked a slow, agonizing death by stoning. She anticipated reprisal if she was discovered. Yet in some place between fear and hope, she reached out to Jesus. The miraculous part is that in the same way Jesus healed this woman, Jesus not only healed me, he took the time to find me and see me. He is doing the same for you. Just as he sees me, he also sees you.

You are navigating the crowd of pain. Move ahead even as fear taunts you. Reach out to Jesus, dear one, and feel healing flow through you as you touch him—fall at his feet, tell your story of how he healed you. Then listen for his words of affirmation: "Well done, Daughter. Well done."

ENCOUNTER GOD

BeLoved, I invite you to come to our safe place where you can rest. Share your anger and pain, pour it out, don't hold back. Lean on me as you release your deepest darkest pain. Pain is a burden you were never meant to carry, so let me carry it for you. Take your time, then pause and listen as I whisper words of life into you.

-Jesus
(Psalm 91; Isaiah 53)

REACHING FOR MORE

You've been uncovered and exposed, pain is ever present and is driving your days and haunting your nights. Only in facing the pain can you move forward and begin to heal. It's risky, hard, and scary, but you can because you aren't alone. Jesus won't take you anywhere you don't want to go, and he knows your limits. If it's too much to answer questions one through three, then pick one question for now and come back later to respond to the other questions. Jesus wants to uncover your pain, to set you on the journey to healing.

1. What is one pain you can face from verbal, emotional, and psychological abuse? Invite Jesus into the pain. Journal: Name the pain, how you were hurt, and what you're feeling. Then ask Jesus what he wants to do with the pain.
2. What is one pain you can face from coercive control? Invite Jesus into the pain. Journal: Name the pain, how you were hurt, and what you're feeling. Then ask Jesus what he wants to do with the pain.
3. What is one pain you can face from sexual abuse? Invite Jesus into the pain. Journal: Name the pain, how you were hurt, and what you're feeling. Then ask Jesus what he wants to do with the pain. Do the same with physical and spiritual abuse. Write as much or as little as you can handle. If you have no words, release your groans to the Holy Spirit.
4. Release the pain to Jesus, imagine him taking it from you. When it's gone, ask Jesus to fill you with the Holy Spirit and imagine being filled with springs of living water. Repeat as often as you want. Write it out as a testament of what he did.
5. Write out how you can be like the woman who took the risk to reach out for more.

CHAPTER 6

UNVEILED

When God's Truth Confronts Your Lies

We use God's mighty weapons, not worldly weapons, to knock down the strongholds of human reasoning and to destroy false arguments.
—2 Corinthians 10:4

One of the greatest battles to be won in our lives is the battle to become fully ourselves and shake loose from the bondage to be what others think we should be.
—Syna Cornelius

I don't recall what led up to all hell breaking loose. I enjoyed a day off from work in the cool of the house. I broke a light in the bathroom while cleaning. Seemed like no big deal, yet for some reason I couldn't breathe as fear filled every part of my body. When Guy came home from his shift, I told him about the broken light as he changed out of his uniform. I expected him to say he'd look at it later, but he went into a frenzy. The next thing I knew, he threw me out of the house.

As I write, memories flood my mind and body, buried emotions escape.

The first night I slept in our pickup. *How did it come to this?* He wouldn't let me back in the house when he left for work that morning. He warned our children not to let me back in the house. They were in junior high school and did what they were told. My emotions ranged from outrage to humiliation. I decided to break the silence and get help. So I walked to a friend's house twice, but she wasn't home. I gave up. The lie was reinforced that I was on my own.

Going to law enforcement wasn't an option. Guy *was* law enforcement. He had made it clear what the consequences would be if I ruined his career and his name. For some unknown reason, I felt responsible to protect him.

I acted as if it was normal to sit out on the steps in the hot summer sun and walk to the gas station to use the bathroom. Slimy and sweaty, I was lost in an ocean of rejection and despondency. My prayers were lost in the abyss of hopelessness, as I knew deep in my soul how screwed up I was.

Guy heard me tell our son I slept in the truck. The smug look on his face as he locked the truck before heading out to work is imprinted on my mind. The second night I slept on the front porch, covered in a sheet to keep the mosquitos off.

In the morning, I gathered what little courage I had to knock on my own door and, on my knees, begged him to let me in to get ready for work. I had called in to work the day before and couldn't miss another day. He relented. The shower was refreshingly sweet, though it was for nothing after I walked 2.6 miles to work on a hot day and, when the day was done, walked back home.

When I arrived home, he again wouldn't let me in the house. I walked away angrily crying, feeling demeaned, and furious at him and God. I walked to a gas station, unsure of what I'd do when I got there. He pulled up with the kids. They got out of the vehicle, and he drove away. He'd asked them if they wanted to stay with him or with me. They chose me. At a loss at what I should do, I called our pastor.

Our pastor picked us up and took us to his home. As we rode along, the kids and I saw Guy in the car next to us. The three of us were filled with terror. *He's looking for us.*

I called my mom the next day and told her what had happened and where we were, but swore her to secrecy. This is one secret I should not have asked her to keep.

Our pastor made it clear we couldn't stay another night, so he drove us home. Our small town didn't have a shelter. The only option was to go back to our house. I was filled with dread as we headed home. When we arrived, Guy was calm and welcoming, telling us how he and the state patrol were looking for us, how worried he was when he couldn't find us, even checking the river. All he did was drive around town looking for us. When he couldn't locate us, he went home and destroyed everything that was precious to me.

He invited the kids to share their feelings. Only my daughter could be honest with him. Though she feared him, she wasn't afraid to speak her mind. While they talked, I scanned the living room, noticing all the things missing.

There was no apology from Guy. We all acted as if it never happened. Life went back to normal, until he handed me a box filled with things precious to me—my baby rattle twisted and broken, my baby dress, tattered and cut up. Twisted emotions flooded my being. I found myself wishing he was dead.

He had, in a sense, exposed me, stripped me naked, humiliated me, and left me for the buzzards to pick clean. I felt powerless, voiceless, loveless, and emotionless.

You can't heal without feeling the pain.

The lies I believed about myself, him, and God burrowed deep within my soul. Believing this was my retribution for the choices I'd made, it never occurred to me that the lies he made me believe weren't true.

You might have memories flooding your mind at the moment. Recollections of experiences that were similar to mine. Did you feel like you brought the abuse on? What emotions bowled you over? Rage, anger, sorrow, grief? Let the feelings flow; don't hold them in. Sweet one, you aren't alone, and as difficult as it is to feel, the emotions won't kill you, though it can feel like they will. You can't heal without feeling the pain. The pain is a reminder that your true self is still alive underneath all the lies.

As I write, I refuse to give the enemy power over me. Years of minimizing the emotions connected to this event passed by before I could let the emotions break free.

I took a break from writing to ask Jesus about this event and the fresh emotions I was feeling as I recounted that story. Though it took place about ten years before I left Guy for good, the realization hit hard—I could have left. My kids were old enough that a judge might have listened to them. A fresh wave of regret rolled over me. All the wasted years.

My story doesn't just make my ex-husband look bad; it makes me look bad too. Which is another tactic of coercive control. How could I turn him in to the police when I believed the lie that I could be implicated in his abuse?

I'm not saying I'm responsible for his behavior. But I lost myself. I don't know when I started protecting him or when I became a willing participant in his abuse by complying and not turning him in to his lieutenant. Abusers systematically tear away our identity, devaluing us until there is nothing left of us.

Domestic abuse takes what should be a loving family and turns father against mother, mother against father, father against children, mother against children, children against parents . . . all to protect the father.

The abuser makes sure you feel responsible to protect him at all costs. But the cost is the freedom of you and your children, while he is free to act however he wants in your home.

TRAUMA BOND

Trauma bonding was first called Stockholm syndrome, when hostages were taken at a bank in 1973. It's defined as an emotional attachment to a captor formed by a hostage, as a result of continuous stress, dependence, and a need to cooperate for survival.[7]

Trauma bonding is how he lured you in. With lies and deception, he tricked you into believing he was someone he wasn't. The abuser creates an emotional attachment in order to gain your trust. Maybe you've experienced it. He may lavish you with words of love, affection, and devotion. He says he's never met anyone like you. He listens to your secrets and learns your boundaries. And you believe him. Then he pushes your boundaries to see how far you'll bend before giving in. If you react negatively, he love bombs you again to distract you from seeing what he did. You become loyal to him, learn to protect him. If you compromise on a boundary, he will make you believe it's your idea, and he may even stop pushing that boundary and look like the hero while you forget all the times he hurt you.

Trauma bonding is calculated and cruel and carries long-term effects. He twisted what you believe to weave a web of lies about your value and worth, twisting the truth about who God is so he could replace God in your life. He holds you there paralyzed until you're completely bonded to him. The real you is obscured behind the webbed veil. And you can't see it happening unless you know what you're looking for. You didn't know you should be wary. No one explains this in the dating handbook. Oh, that's right. There *is* no handbook on how to spot a predator.

> **Jesus said, "The thief's purpose is to steal and kill and destroy. My purpose is to give them a rich and satisfying life."**

YOU HAVE AN ENEMY

In John 10:10, Jesus said, "The thief's purpose is to steal and kill and destroy. My purpose is to give them a rich and satisfying life."

Much like your abuser, Satan lies to you about every event in your life. He distorts the meaning of both good and bad events, casting blame where it doesn't exist. Satan's lies are covert and subtle, designed to hit you at the core of who you are, who others are, and who you believe God is or isn't. His lies become your truth and can be fueled by the abuse you've endured. Satan, the enemy of your soul, will reinforce the lies, using the people you love the most until the lies you believe become your truth.

But as we walk through the lies you've been told by both your abuser and Satan, remember Jesus understands. Satan lied to him too.

As Jesus hung on the cross, the sounds of jeering rose through the air. The curious wanted to know if he was the Messiah, wondering why he didn't save himself. What Jesus heard and saw wasn't just the sounds and sights of the people. He heard and saw his enemies, the unseen forces of evil. They surrounded Jesus, gleeful as they watched him die, believing they had finally won. Jesus felt abandoned as the hounds of hell surrounded him and hurled lies of rejection, abandonment, hatred, and hopelessness. He yelled, "My God, my God, why have you abandoned me?" (Matthew 27:46). He was beaten, battered, bruised, and naked. Jesus was physically, verbally, and emotionally abused. He knows and understands what you have experienced and feel. Love stood against evil and won. And you can too.

STRONGHOLDS

You may not realize how much of your life is a lie. Abusers twist every word they say to you and about you, every episode becomes your fault, every action they take is twisted to make them look like the hero or victim. The lies they form around and about you create strongholds and a veil so that you can't see reality. This veil needs to be removed so you can see the truth about who God says you are and so you can be who he created you to be before the foundation of the world.

Strongholds are deceptions and lies we believe. Satan uses places of weakness inside us to stand and attack us. He is the deceiver and slanderer. He lies *to* you and *about* you in order to destroy you.

You and I tend to create walls of self-protection, believing a false version of ourselves to deaden the pain of the lie. We pretend all is well, when it's an illusion. The illusion keeps you in an incessant cycle of lies and self-protection. The way you self-protect becomes your source to find truth, security, and comfort. Your false version of you can't call out to God which leaves the real you starving. You wonder why nothing changes and why you don't hear God or why your prayers don't seem to go anywhere. There's a reason for that. As strange as it sounds, the same walls you raised to preserve and protect yourself also create a barrier to God's voice. And when you can't hear God's voice, it's hard to hear the truth about who God is and who we are.

> The same walls you raised to preserve and protect yourself also create a barrier to God's voice.

You and I often end up believing, *This is just the way I am.* What if it's not? What if you've been living this way for so long you can't tell lies from the truth of who God says you are? If you don't know who you are in Christ, you won't recognize what's true and what isn't true.

What must I do to be accepted? What if being seen is dangerous?

When I protected myself, others reacted negatively. Maybe they, too, were operating out of the distorted version of themselves. I experienced fear, rejection, pride, shame, anger, unforgiveness, depression, trauma, and more. I was offended when these people reacted.

As you go about your business, self-protecting and bumping up against people, their reactions can validate your truth, which reinforces the lies you believe, leading to more self-protection, which causes more reactions. The pain burns deeper and deeper into your soul until it creates a well-worn vinyl record; the needle gets stuck and keeps playing the same song over and over in your life until you agree with Satan's lies about you.

But the enemy's biggest lie is his distortion of who God is. He taunts you with thoughts such as, God could have stopped what happened, but he didn't. God is in control and can take care of those he loves, so he must not have loved you. Because God is all knowing and all present and loves us, the enemy's lies seem valid. Yet God isn't a puppet master, pulling strings and causing bad things to happen to us to make us stronger and super Christians.

Why *do* bad things happen? I don't know. Some say it's because you made bad choices or others made bad choices that harmed you. The answer is, you have an enemy who hates you, his only desire is to see God's beloved destroyed by whatever means necessary.

When you and I are in a place of deception, we judge ourselves and believe we're bad, worthless, and unlovable. It's our truth, at times. But it's not *the* truth. Here is the Bible's simplified version of how to break strongholds: "The moment one turns to the Lord with an open heart, the veil is lifted and they see" (2 Corinthians 3:16 TPT).

We're reminded to take our thoughts captive in 2 Corinthians 10:5, as if our thoughts are the bad guys and they are being arrested, convicted, and thrown in prison. We don't do this in our own power and strength. It is only through spiritual warfare, submitting our thoughts to Jesus, that the lies can be unwrapped so we can hear truth. Jesus will never condemn us. If your thoughts appear to condemn you, that is the voice of the great deceiver. But it takes knowing the voice of Jesus, which you learn through reading Scripture and using discernment, to know whose voice you're hearing.

COME MEET THE MAN

Part of God's plan all along was to destroy the work of the enemy in our lives, even before the cross. In John 4:7–38, we read the story of the woman at the well.

It seemed as if she went through men like babies go through diapers. She had five husbands and was living with another man at the time she met Jesus. You may have read her story and judged her as I did. I assumed something was wrong with her. Then God planted a thought in my mind by reminding me what life must have been like for her.

This Samaritan woman, as Scripture describes her, was half Jewish. She was considered by Jews to be "lower than low." She most likely married young. What happened with the first husband? Did he throw her out? Did he decide he didn't want her anymore? Did he give her to another man just to be rid of her? Did he die? I assumed she had choices, but she most likely didn't. She lived in a patriarchal and misogynistic time when women were considered property and were often oppressed.

Fathers determined who and when their daughters married. You see how the cycle probably played out in her life. Tossed out like garbage by her first husband, she was picked up by a second, third, fourth, and fifth husband, and the last husband may not have given her a legal divorce, so she couldn't marry the current guy. She saw herself as damaged goods, each time discarded. Imagine the lies she believed about her identity: valueless, worthless, trash.

By the time she met Jesus, she was a social outcast, yet Jesus loved her enough to stop for a drink at the well in the heat of the day, knowing she would be there. With every deflection she made, he brought her back to him and what he offered—complete satisfaction in *him*. He revealed his identity to her.

Her encounter with Jesus transformed her. When the disciples showed up, she felt their displeasure. I imagine her eyes locked on

Jesus, experiencing his love and tenderness as she processed the revelation of who he is.

The moment it struck her—he's the long-awaited Messiah—she didn't waver. Scripture says she dropped her empty jug, and rushed to the people who despised her to tell them of the man she had just met. That amazes me. What it tells me is that she was overwhelmed by the love of Jesus. In their interaction, lies were broken, truth was revealed about God, Jesus, and herself. Yet that's what love does. Her life changed that day. Jesus pursued her. He saw the woman the people scorned and men used, and he loved her. She discarded dignity and rushed into the town to the very people who rejected and shunned her. And get this: They all listened to what she said and came running out to meet Jesus. This woman who was a nobody to everybody became a somebody the day she met Jesus! She was never the same; she followed the one who is love.

> You, my amazing friend, are a *but God* story. You thought you were worthless and unwanted, *but God* showed you otherwise.

Many have speculated what happened to her after her encounter with Jesus. John may not have known her name, but Jesus did. And he trusted her with *his* name, when he told her (before telling anyone else), "I am Messiah." Can you imagine? A woman who the world discarded was the person Jesus saw as worthy enough to be the first to know that the long-awaited Messiah had come.

BUT GOD

You, my amazing friend, are a *but God* story. You thought you were worthless and unwanted, *but God* showed you otherwise. Jesus's love for you is as deep as it is wide. Though it feels like he abandoned you, he didn't. The lies of the enemy have been shouting at you, drowning out God's whispers of love and the invitation of living water. Like the woman at the well, you too can experience the truth about who Jesus truly is, about who we are in him. "He rescued me from the mighty waters and drew me to himself" (Psalm 18:16 TPT).

You started this chapter considering you may not be who you

think you are, identifying lies, embracing the truth. I am thrilled you're willing to embrace the truth, face the pain, and allow Jesus to remove the veil of lies and deception. Well done, Daughter. Well done.

ENCOUNTER GOD

BeLoved, I will remove the veil of lies and deception that distorts how you see yourself and me. Though I know your every thought, I want to hear what you have to say. As you release the words, they will lose their power over you. I am with you in the darkness. I will never betray or leave you alone. You, dear one, are so precious to me.

-Jesus
(Psalm 139; Isaiah 41:10)

REACHING FOR MORE

Satan, the father of lies, can keep you from healing by creating strongholds through the lies you believe about God, you, and your ex-husband. One thing to remember is that Satan will always lie to you about everything. God will always tell you the truth about everything. He will removed the veil of lies so that you can see clearly.

1. If you're able, write out one incident from your marriage that stands out as the most atrocious. (You can write it out in brief bullet points or as a longer story.) Ask Jesus to show you the lies that came out of that incident. Then ask him what the truth is.
2. Ask Jesus to remove the veil so you can see the lies you believe about who you are.

3. Ask Jesus what the truth is for each lie you wrote down about yourself.

4. How has abuse twisted your view of God, and what lies do you believe about him?

5. Ask Jesus to show you the truth about the character of God.

PART 3

OVERCOMER

Learning to Live Until You're Alive

By now you've confronted the whys, pain, and lies by choosing to overcome everything you thought you believed about your abuser, yourself, and God.

You were crushed to the point of despair. You were gaslighted until you thought you were crazy. And when you finally got out, you were pursued and held captive by beliefs that weren't your own. But not any longer.

It's time to triumph over the stigma of domestic violence and divorce. It's time to really walk out your freedom, discover the goodness of God, and reframe how you see yourself and God as you break the power and control your husband had over you.

Welcome to freedom, baby! It is glorious.

"Guide my steps by your word, so I will not be overcome by evil" (Psalm 119:133).

CHAPTER 7

UNWAVERING

Break Out of Prison and Overcome Deception

Some of us once sat in darkness, living in the dark shadows of death. We were prisoners to our pain, chained to our regrets.

—Psalm 107:10 (TPT)

But they're walking on a path to nowhere, wandering away into deeper deception.

—Proverbs 2:15 (TPT)

Who would have thought I would ever address a room full of men who had recently come out of prison for crimes that sent shivers up my spine?

At the time, I was on the board of directors for a local ministry that was investigating a process to help women coming out of sex trafficking and abuse. Another organization that helped men rehabilitate after coming out of prison agreed to share its process and resources with our ministry. I learned a lot that day.

If the male inmates were approved, they would go directly from prison into transitional housing to grow in their faith and have accountability to not repeat their crimes. The organization that sought to help us invited our board members to participate in their day of ministry provided for their men. It allowed us to interact and talk with the men. At the end of the ministry day, each of us was given time to share how the day impacted us.

Listening to one man after another get up to talk about the power of the time they had just experienced was both exciting and awkward.

I had nothing in common with these men—they were convicted felons. I wondered what I could say that wouldn't sound shallow or condemning since I had never been in prison. God crashed into my thoughts and reminded me that I had been in prison with bars made of shame, fear, insecurity, and pain. When it was my turn to share, I jumped out of my chair. Scanning the room, I released the words about my prison of domestic abuse. I saw a *knowing* in their eyes as I told the story of *my* prison and, "Oh, by the way . . . he was a cop."

Most of us, at one time or another, have spent time in a prison of our own making. We may not live behind *physical* bars, but we're still trapped. Some of the men I talked with looked and acted like prisoners. Their shame over what they were and where they came from was evident in their demeanor. Some had been out long enough that they didn't look or act like prisoners. Some had been in prison more than once for the same violation. And for some, prison life was all they knew, and they were like little children, set free of boundaries, giddy with excitement.

There was always the pull of their past, yet they yearned to break free from the prison mindset—to know there was a time they could have made a different choice. Because of their choices, the ankle monitor was a constant reminder of the limitations to their freedom, their shame, and what they were.

Where they were emotionally is not all that different from where those of us who have experienced emotional bars find ourselves.

Our pasts will likely haunt us, and Satan will try to lay the blame on us for what we have experienced. The enemy of our souls wants to keep us bound as a prisoner, locked in the cycle of darkness. While the prisoners had done something to deserve their imprisonment and reminders of their past, we who are innocent often walk around with our ankle monitors to limit us and keep us from freedom and remind us that we are trapped in shame and condemnation.

But there is one who is powerful enough to release us from our pasts. In his days on earth, Jesus was often dismissed as just the local boy putting on airs (see Luke 4:14–30).

You may make the same mistake as Jesus's contemporaries and

believe he is powerless in the face of abuse. That thought or belief is the beginning of deception. Jesus came to give life, to heal, to release the captives and prisoners, to make the spiritually and physically blind see. He has the power to help, and he's willing to help. Will you let him?

UNRAVELING UNWORTHINESS

Part of our struggle as abused women is reaching the point where we can believe God is willing to help. Unworthiness is a close cousin of shame. We've been judged, found deficient, lacking, and unwanted. Unworthiness flows from Satan's deception about who Jesus is and who you are to him. Our abusers and Satan deceive us into believing we are worthless, your abuser sees you as a possession, and the only value you hold for him is what you can do for him.

The word *deceive* is the shiftier and craftier cousin of *lie*. It means to trick or lie, to purposely cause you to believe something that isn't true, betraying you, leading you astray, misleading you. Deception is a powerful weapon of Satan. Deception takes the rejection caused by your abuse and twists it to say, *You are unworthy, unwanted, unloved.* In that mindset you may be tempted to turn from God and believe he is the source of your pain, that he is the one rejecting you.

> Deception takes the rejection caused by your abuse and twists it to say, *You are unworthy, unwanted, unloved.*

Feeling unworthy impacts every area of our lives, causing us to waver in our identity and faith. We begin to believe we are unfit, guilty, a fraud, and vile. If you look back on your life, you may be able to see how you made decisions based on those beliefs.

I reached out to a few friends and asked them to describe how their lives and choices were impacted by believing they were unworthy. Here are their responses:

- "I didn't believe I deserved healing. When I feel unworthy, a common loop runs through my mind: *No one will think I'm worth fighting for, protecting, believing in.* I even ascribed those tapes to God. It makes me feel hopeless, and what's the point? I have suicidal thoughts at times around these tapes, much less than I used to, but they're still there. I've never stopped pursuing Jesus, but unworthiness has colored my perception of what he wants for me. It's been quite the journey to believe my life matters and I can have good things."

- "Feeling unworthy kept me from healing, because I'd been beaten down. The lack of self-esteem . . . and Satan told me I didn't deserve happiness or freedom. I felt unworthy, not only from my abusive ex-husband but also from religious leaders, because I grew up in a cult. God was presented as far away, unreachable, judgmental, and angry. Everything was works-based, and the goal was perfection. I was taught God wouldn't love me if I didn't do _____ or did do _____. Fear kept me from pursuing Jesus—fear of not being worthy of his love, and not fully being able to believe unconditional love was possible. I'd rarely experienced it."

- "Feeling unworthy kept me from experiencing healing. My behavior was centered on escaping the pain, not dealing with it. When I believed I was unworthy, I saw myself as a hypocrite because my thoughts, my heart, and my actions did not line up. I beat myself up on the inside. I saw everything that wasn't right as my fault . . . I was bad or wrong or faulty in some way. That felt ugly and dirty. I wanted to run away from myself, but I couldn't. Subconsciously I created the person I wished I was and stuffed the ugliness I didn't want anyone to see deep inside. I did not feel like Jesus would want to talk to me. Or worse, I was afraid if he did I would only hear how wrong/bad/disobedient I was. I was confused and had questions. I felt he would be angry that I didn't have enough faith. When I heard preachers talk about the Scripture that says 'Without faith, it is impossible to please God,' I would think, *There is no way I can please God.* With every thought of reaching out in hope, the enemy would knock me down with this Scripture and others like it."

There's a beautiful story recorded in Luke 7:36–50 of a woman who discovered her worth in Jesus. Remember in biblical times women's options were limited. Women didn't have rights or a voice, their only value was as a wife and mother. Also, men could divorce or discard their wives for the smallest reason, but women could not divorce or leave their husbands. Men would illegally divorce their wives, leaving them unable to remarry. If an abandoned woman's family didn't take her back, her options were few, leading some women to make a living by selling their bodies for food and lodging.

One day Jesus was invited to the home of Simon, a Pharisee, to dine with other religious leaders. That was when *she* walked into the room.

This woman entered the room carrying a beautiful alabaster jar. She was bold and unwavering as she walked up to Jesus. She knelt and began washing his feet with her tears, using her hair to wipe away the dirt. She poured the expensive perfume over his feet as she continued to kiss his feet over and over.

Stunned into silence, the religious leaders watched in horror.

She wasn't just any woman, she was *that* woman. Simon the Pharisee probably knew her. Although she is nameless in Scripture, she was known in the room as "a certain immoral woman" (Luke 7:37).

She was considered bad to the bone.

She dared to walk into the home of a Pharisee—who strictly and harshly kept religious law. He would sooner stone her to death than let her into his home. Gutsy. She didn't hesitate, didn't think, she just walked into the lair of those who used and condemned her. Yet she had nothing to lose and everything to gain.

The men looked at her and back to Jesus to see his reaction. Though they didn't say the words, Jesus knew what they were thinking: *Wow. People say Jesus is a prophet. If he is, he would know what kind of woman she is.*

Jesus addressed Simon, telling him a story and asking him a question about who would be more grateful: the one forgiven for much or little. Jesus acknowledged that the woman's sins were many. Yet Jesus told her, "Your sins are forgiven. . . . Your faith has saved [healed and freed] you; go in peace" (Luke 7:48, 50).

The woman who walked out of the house was not the same woman who walked in. She entered in worthless and walked out worthy. She became a new woman; the old was gone. She was no longer a nobody. She had been transformed into a daughter of the King.

That story leads me to believe that the woman and Jesus had a previous encounter. Her act revealed her gratitude as she poured out her extravagant love on him. She'd made choices based on her belief that she was unworthy to be anything but what she was. I believe Jesus changed how she saw herself—as one worthy of love. That may be what gave her the boldness to walk into the home of a Pharisee and anoint Jesus with her most valuable possession.

Someone may have named her unworthy, but Jesus renamed her worthy.

> The next time the enemy tells you that you're unworthy, stand unwavering in the belief of who you are as a daughter of the King.

The father of lies wants to keep you oppressed in the deception, feeling unworthy of Jesus through your shame and fear. Unworthiness causes you not to believe in God's love, to believe God is twisted and cruel and that he is the one who caused your abuse. That simply isn't true. He is reaching out to you and offering freedom. The next time the enemy tells you that you're unworthy, stand unwavering in the belief of who you are as a daughter of the King.

HOW ABUSE TWISTED SCRIPTURE

I have always loved to learn, study, and teach what I know, especially the Word of God. Back when I was still dealing with the imprisonment of my abuse, I didn't understand how my past twisted how I read the Bible and how I saw God and understood biblical principles. We've talked about how the enemy uses deception to lie to us about who we are and who God is. Deception does that by blurring what we see and how we hear.

What I saw and heard in the Bible is part of what kept me in an abusive marriage for thirty years. I left the marriage even though I believed God would be angry with me. But looking back, he was clearly telling me to go. In order for us to stand unwavering in our belief about who God is, we need to reconcile what we know he's told us to do and what some Christians have asked us to do or not do.

Currently many churches believe there are only two reasons for divorce—abandonment and infidelity. If he walks out on you or cheats on you, according to most church bylaws you are free to seek a divorce.

He is free to walk out on you but you're not free to walk out on an abusive marriage. As long as he just watches porn and doesn't cheat, then he's good and you're bound to him (note the sarcasm). Let's look at the definitions of the two words.

Infidelity doesn't just mean marital disloyalty, unfaithfulness, and adultery. It's also a breach of your trust, a disloyal act, transgression which is violating the law. Infidelity isn't just adultery, it's the very definition of abuse.

Abandonment is when he leaves completely by walking out and never returning, forsaking you utterly; he gives up, and withdraws from you. He is careless, reckless, and unrestrained in how he treats you. Rejects you, invalidates you, and bends you to his will. You can live in the same home, be married, and still be abandoned.

Too many churches take a narrow view of infidelity and abandonment in order to protect marriage at any cost.

I was a young believer in Bible college when I learned about God's view of divorce in a class on 1 Corinthians. My professor talked about how bad divorce is, how God hates divorce, implying those who divorce were somehow lesser Christians. The more he talked, the more angry I became. I exploded, "My mom is one of the godliest women I know, she's divorced, and you're saying she's not good enough!" The entire class just looked at me. The professor was shocked that I challenged him. I don't remember what else I said or what happened after my outburst. I only remember how I felt from the implication of his words . . . your mom is less than other believers because she's divorced.

The message was loud and clear: God hates divorce. We often hear Scripture twisted to support abuse. The Scriptures now give me hope as I heal, but while I was in the throes of abuse, I perceived Scripture, especially the following verses, entirely differently.

"Of course, you get no credit for being patient if you are beaten for doing wrong. But if you suffer for doing good and endure it patiently, God is pleased with you" (1 Peter 2:20).

"God blesses those who patiently endure testing and temptation. Afterward they will receive the crown of life that God has promised to those who love him" (James 1:12).

"We are pressed on every side by troubles, but we are not crushed [But I *am* crushed]. We are perplexed, but not driven to despair [I am in despair]. We are hunted down, but never abandoned by God [Then where is he?]. We get knocked down, but we are not destroyed [But I am. There's nothing left of me]. Through suffering, our bodies continue to share in the death of Jesus so that the life of Jesus may also be seen in our bodies [So when he abuses me, I'm suffering with Jesus?]" (2 Corinthians 4:8–10).

The message was loud and clear: abuse is suffering for Jesus.

Those are just a few verses that I interpreted as meaning, *This is your life, patiently endure, and you'll get a crown one day.* As I healed, I could see how the enemy had twisted Scripture. Now I can see through the lens of healing that these Scriptures aren't endorsing abuse but are a source of comfort as I heal.

Other verses seemed to tell me I needed to stay married so that I could win my husband to Jesus. One example is 1 Peter 3:1–6, especially verses 1–2: "They will be won over by observing your pure and reverent lives."

At church I'd listen to messages about couples struggling in their marriages and how the husband would surrender to Jesus. I heard, "Hold on to God's promises, and your husband will change." And hold on I did, to the detriment of my children. Guy "came to Jesus" many times in the marriage, but his behavior never changed. I prayed harder and longer after reading books on how to be a better wife. Unfortunately, many of these included suggestions such as wrap yourself in plastic wrap and welcome him home from work, give him more sex and you'll win him over, and similar ideas.

The message was loud and clear: it was my obligation to win him to Jesus.

Again the enemy twisted this Scripture to make me believe I was responsible to win my husband over to Jesus. Reading the Scripture today, in light of my current healthy marriage, and including with it verse 7, which speaks of a husband's responsibility, I see there are times when Tom and I may disagree on something, so we should set it aside and both of us pray that God would bring us to agreement. (See also 1 Corinthians 7:5.)

Then there are the Scriptures I gladly live out with my husband, Tom, in a healthy relationship where we mutually honor, respect, and love. During my abuse, however, I read these same verses as saying I needed to submit to Guy's abuse, but that isn't the message of these words.

"For wives, this means submit to your husbands as to the Lord. For a husband is the head of his wife as Christ is the head of the church" (Ephesians 5:22–23).

"So you wives should submit to your husbands in everything [Even abuse?]" (Ephesians 5:24).

"The wife must respect her husband [Even though he doesn't deserve it?]" (Ephesians 5:33).

The message was loud and clear: you do whatever your husband says or suffer the consequences.

If you believe the messages as I did, it may be because your view of God is skewed as mine was.

Abuse Deceptively Says	The Truth Is
God loves marriage more than he loves me.	God loves you more than he hates anything (Isaiah 54:10).
Men are more important than women.	God created man and woman in his image (Genesis 1:27).
Women have no rights in marriage.	We submit to one another (Ephesians 5:21); husbands are to love their wives, just as Jesus loves the church and sees her as glorious (Ephesians 5:25–28); husbands are to honor their wives (1 Peter 3:7).

Abuse Deceptively Says	The Truth Is
God is okay with abuse since he allows it to happen.	God isn't okay with abuse. He rescued Israel from abuse (Exodus 2:24–25; 3:7–9), and he is close to the brokenhearted (Psalm 34:18).

I have good news. These twists of Scripture are straight from the pit of hell. The message of abuse is meant to deceive you and twist what you know about the Bible—the slanderer knows Scripture probably better than you do, but twists it to fit his purposes . . . to turn you from the only one who can help you overcome and break free of abuse and deception. Satan twisted the Word when he tempted Jesus in the wilderness. He uses the same tactic on you. Jesus, who is the Truth and the Word, defeated Satan with both the spoken and the written Word. You can too!

Ephesians 5 is a beautiful picture of what marriage should look like.

Each Scripture that I quoted is a reminder that God does share in our suffering, that he knows pain and betrayal, that he promises to see us through the agony of healing. Ephesians 5 is a beautiful picture of what marriage should look like. Hold on to the verses as an emblem of hope.

OVERCOMING BROKENNESS

You've experienced the worst kind of brokenness through coercion, threats, and control. Brokenness meant to destroy you. God wants to take you on a pilgrimage to healing through brokenness so you can learn to live as a free daughter of God.

Read Song of Songs 2:10–15 at BibleGateway.com in The Passion Translation. Read it again, slowly. Let every word soak into you. Add your name as you read it once more.

Again, Song of Songs is more than the romantic story of King Solomon and his bride. It's the romance of the Bridegroom—Jesus—and his bride—you.

As I read the King's words to me, I heard:

Get up and get moving, my dear Karen, my darling girl. I'm calling you into my heart. Trust me to lead you into healing. It's time, beautiful one. It's the season of healing. It's time to leave the barrenness of your winter; it's time to come out of hiding behind your pain. The seed of your pain will produce the most beautiful flowers. It's time for you to blossom, for singing, for pruning. Songs of healing are breaking out; the music will carry you forward.

Can you feel it? It's the day of your destiny. You will see me bring purpose out of your pain. No one can stop my plans for you. Bringing purpose out of your pain is a sweet fragrance to me, and I see who you are. So, dear one, get ready for change. My beautiful one, run with me, rise above the pain. It's time for you to move, to become an overcomer. I am taking you up into my secret place. I long to hear your sweet voice call out to me when it gets difficult. Radiate my love and glory. Your worship is a perfume to me.

Take captive the thoughts and lies that keep you from me. Those lies are insidious and keep you trapped and begin eating away at all I've planted in you. Are you willing to cut away the lies? I promise we will do it together.

Love,
Your Bridegroom

Allow God to break through the lies, knock down walls of self-protection, and shatter the hardness around your heart, so you can overcome your past and step into your future. Overcoming the past doesn't mean acting as if it never happened. I tried that. It doesn't work. What I suppressed in the day came out in my dreams.

The enemy wants to keep you locked in the prison of bondage, to hold you accountable for what Jesus has already paid for. The men from the beginning of the chapter were required to wear an ankle monitor as a reminder they aren't completely free, even though they are out of prison. Jesus has so completely freed you from prison that it's as if you were never in prison.

Overcoming means you've gained victory, you've prevailed over your past. We do that by facing the past head-on. We drive into a

When the new is created, it is simply beautiful.

forest fire, through a flooded road, and crawl through the desert of all that was done to us.

As you surrender, you become transformed. A caterpillar must dissolve into mush before it becomes a butterfly. Surrender to the mush, which means dissolving all the old before the new can be created. But when the new is created, it is simply beautiful. Open your brand-new wings to the world and fly into freedom. Doesn't new sound inviting?

ENCOUNTER GOD

BeLoved, you can trust the truth of my Word. It's time to break free from the power of deception and to immerse yourself in me. Darkness can't stand against my light. I am the one who creates roads through the wilderness and rivers in the desert. I am the one who makes all things new. Just watch and see what I will do!

~The one who loves you
(John 1:5; Isaiah 43:18–19)

REACHING FOR MORE

Your husband misled you about who he is, and throughout your marriage he used persuasion to minimize and deny that you were experiencing abuse by blaming you for his behavior. Everything he did was designed to leave you feeling unworthy of anything or anyone but him. It's time to be unwavering and break through the cloud of deception into the clarity of truth.

1. Looking back over your marriage, can you now see the deception? If so, list the incidents that stand out to you. If not, ask Jesus to show you, then list each one. Leave space after each

and go back and write out the truth. If you can't see the truth, ask Jesus to show you the truth.

2. List all the ways your husband made you feel unworthy. Leave room to add to the list and space to write out both what Jesus says and the Scripture that negates what your husband said or did.

3. List out the Scriptures or "Christian" sayings that caused you to believe God was okay with abuse.

4. Write out the truth about those same Scriptures. If you're not sure, ask Jesus to show you the truth about his Word.

5. Go back and read the letter from the Bridegroom in Song of Songs 2:10–15, adding your name. How do you feel as you read? If you want, read it again and again until you believe it.

CHAPTER 8

UNASHAMED

Determine to Live Out Loud

Fear not; you will no longer live in shame. Don't be afraid; there is no more disgrace for you. You will no longer remember the shame of your youth and the sorrows of widowhood.
—Isaiah 54:4

My friend Cindy remembers what I was like when I first moved to Texas.

She remembers the fear and emptiness in my eyes. I didn't stand up straight, my shoulders were slumped forward. "You rarely made eye contact with me," Cindy said. "You acted as if you did not want to be noticed or even acknowledged. Your voice was quiet and your manner was timid. I remember being surprised by the way you acted until later when you told me your story; then it all made sense."

What Cindy saw that day was my constant companion—shame. Shame shielded me from prying eyes that might see the secrets I hid within.

WHAT IS SHAME?

My New Living Translation Bible concordance describes shame as "a condition or feeling of humiliating disgrace or disrepute; something that brings censure and reproach." We could stop right here and not say another word about shame. Like me, you may have felt the weight of those words—memories may be flooding your mind of the most humiliating moments in your marriage or while dating.

Shame hides in the dark, where it does its most destructive work. Shame reinforces the lies that we believe about ourselves and distorts our view of God. In my story, my ex-husband didn't want to carry his shame so he heaped his shame and pain on me to carry. No wonder the pain and shame were unbearable; they weren't mine to bear at all.

Shame kept me silent and trapped in the marriage, not wanting anyone to know our horror story. Shame became my best friend and worst enemy, conspiring to keep me trapped in a cage of my own making.

But my greatest shame was that, by staying in the marriage, I didn't protect my children. I was completely broken by the time they were teens. Controlled by fear, I couldn't and sometimes wouldn't protect them from Guy's rage. The memories still bring tears and sorrow. It is the one *if only* that still haunts me.

Please hold on and bear with me as we look at this horrible five-letter word: shame.

By the end of this chapter, I hope that you'll feel different than you do at this moment, that you will know you can begin living out loud instead of silenced by shame. I would remind you how much your heavenly Father loves you. At any moment, when shame begins shouting, you tell it to be silent. Romans 8:1 is a powerful reminder: "So now there is no condemnation for those who belong to Christ Jesus."

The Look of Shame

Shame looks like pushing people away. It looks like putting our shame on others. Shame looks like hiding, manipulating, controlling. It looks like perfectionism. It looks like performance. It looks like giving up. It looks like prison. It looks like sabotage. It looks like disconnection. It looks like blame. It looks like rules. It looks like hurting others. It grows with fear.

Shame changes the way that you see. It whispers lies that twist how you see yourself, God, and others. It changes how you see your circumstances. Shame keeps you from seeing God's love and goodness.

The Feel of Shame

Shame feels heavy and numb. It feels icky and dirty. It feels like rejection, not belonging, being unseen, invisible. It feels as if it's eating you alive. It feels normal. It feels like giving up. It feels irrational. It feels like chaos. It feels like fear.

Shame keeps you from feeling God's presence. It keeps you from feeling love from God and others. Shame changes how you feel.

The Sound of Shame

Shame sounds like comparison. It sounds negative. It sounds empty, like clanging bells in a hollow hallway. It sounds like jokes, putdowns, swearing, nagging, lecturing, and sarcasm. It sounds critical. It sounds loud, silent, brash. It sounds like talking too much. It sounds like a know-it-all. It sounds like fear.

Shame sounds flat and shallow. It sounds unstable, illogical, and careless. It sounds irresponsible. Shame changes how you hear.

The Behavior of Shame

Shame acts like you're inadequate and don't care. It acts religious, agnostic, or atheistic. It acts like you're better than others. It acts like hurting others. It acts like depression. It acts shallow. It acts insecure and selfish. It acts like fear.

Shame acts like defeat, pretense, and phoniness. Shame changes you.

The Lies of Shame

Shame says, "You are bad; you are wrong; and it's all your fault." Shame says, "You're unworthy of love and goodness." Shame says, "You'll never change—this is your life, so accept it."

What if shame is a liar?

WHEN SHAME ENTERED THE WORLD

In Genesis 3, we discover that shame hid in the garden of Eden, waiting for the perfect moment to blame and shift its shame to Woman (just a note that Woman was actually the name of the first woman). Salivating as he waited, Shame allowed himself to be seen now and again, speaking to her . . . speaking about her. He knew her curiosity would get the best of her.

When the right moment came, the first woman stood before two trees. Shame hid in the tree of knowledge, engaging Woman in polite conversation, appealing to her with kindness, captivating her with his charm. Wrapped in the body of a serpent, we assume he was ugly and repulsive. But what if he was a beautiful creature? If he had been repulsive, would she have listened to him or continued to chat with him?

Then one day he asked a question, "Did God really say . . . ?"

He offered her what already belonged to her—wisdom, knowledge, and to be like God—while failing to mention that with knowledge came evil. She bit into the luscious fruit, chewing as she offered a taste to her husband, Adam. But the moment she swallowed, she knew she'd been deceived.

Imagine the shame washing over her as Adam blamed her for their choice to eat from the Tree of Knowledge of Good and Evil. Shame drove Adam and Woman to hide, cover up, and blame one another. Listen to how the dialogue ensued (Genesis 3:9–13):

God: "Where are you?"
Adam: "I heard you walking in the garden, so I hid. I was afraid because I was naked."
God: "Who told you that you were naked? Have you eaten from the tree whose fruit I commanded you not to eat?"
Adam: "It was the woman you gave me who gave me the fruit, and I ate it."
God: "What have you done?"
Woman: "The serpent deceived me. That's why I ate it."

God cursed the beautiful creature and turned him into a hideous slithering serpent and put shame back on him, where it belonged. Jesus put shame back on the fallen one, once and for all, when he died on the cross. "In this way, he disarmed the spiritual rulers and authorities. He shamed them publicly by his victory over them on the cross" (Colossians 2:15).

God didn't curse or shame Adam or Woman. They were given consequences, not curses. God cursed the ground (in Texas, that means weeds, stickers, and fire ants).

God offered hope, not shame, to Adam and Woman. I imagine God picked the most beautiful animal to sacrifice to design clothes to cover them. God sent them from the only home they knew, not out of punishment, but for redemption. How do we know it wasn't punishment? Because the woman's name became Eve, the Hebrew word for *life*. Adam no longer blamed her. How do we know? After they had eaten the fruit, Adam named her . . . Eve, the mother of life.

Shame keeps us from God, our source of comfort and forgiveness. Shame destroys, distorts, shatters, and hides. God restores our life and mends our soul to give us clarity and revelation. Healthy shame or guilt draws us to repentance and healing; toxic shame drives us from relationship.

> Healthy shame or guilt draws us to repentance and healing; toxic shame drives us from relationship.

The question is, "Who told you that you were unworthy, unloved, unseen?"

Even though you aren't standing in front of the serpent, he's still talking and condemning you. His words sound right. Just enough truth to sound like God or yourself, reminding you of who you aren't. Reinforcing the belief that you are unworthy.

I believed God was mean and angry, ready to punish me for my mistakes. I was a disappointment to God, so why should he bother with me anyway? I committed the sin of all sins, according to some churches' twisting of Malachi 2:16, by seeking a divorce.

It didn't matter that Guy was aggressive, combative, and controlling. Or that shame thrived on our secrets and isolation. I felt the accusations from some women at church that I was weak and flawed because I allowed this to happen to me. They assumed if it was that bad I could have left the marriage, or maybe I even asked for the abuse.

HIDDEN SHAME

After I left and started to heal, I was able to cut away bits of the shame. But it would take more years before I could see that shame had embedded itself in my life. I often thought, *It's just the way I am.*

> We can cut shame off like a noxious plant, but . . . if we don't dig shame out by the roots, it will return with a vengeance.

Shame hides and disguises itself. It doesn't want to be found. It's like a vine that attaches to another plant, winding around and around until it becomes one with the plant.

Shame is attached to the pain we avoid and the lies we believe. We can cut shame off like a noxious plant, but if we don't change our thinking about what we believe, if we don't dig shame out by the roots, it will return with a vengeance.

Shame had me believing I wasn't enough, that other women had what I longed for, that they were prettier, thinner, and more talented. That tape repeated itself in my mind until I thought it was truth. I held myself to a standard I couldn't live up to. When I gave voice to my standards, it landed on the women around me as judgment. Like Adam, I pointed to others and shamed them too.

I have always felt I needed to lose ten pounds. When I would say that aloud, women who were heavier than me would feel judgment from me. One woman said to me, "Do you hold us all to your standard?" I didn't, but I did. It was never my intention, yet my pebble landed on other women like a boulder.

I believed that if I looked good I had value. That lie was at the core of who I thought I was. It's a lie I have battled in my mind most of my life. Yes, I know who I am in Christ—I'm his BeLoved daughter. My value is based on what he has done for me and in me. Yet when I see another woman walking out her purpose, the first thought in my head is, *Why not me? Lord, you know I'm not getting any younger.*

When those thoughts come, and they do, you not only can cast them out but you also can take them captive and say *No!* Begin to speak life, blessing, and favor over yourself. If God will do all he's doing for others, he will do it for you too. When you begin to think, *Why not me?* the enemy will try to take you back to the lies you once believed. That's when it's up to you to do your part and say *No!* Just because the thought comes doesn't mean you should hang on to it.

Pride can keep us trapped in abuse, pain, and shame, and keep us from healing. Pride is the disguise of shame and is triggered by fear.

Let me explain. In the church, divorce has for many years produced shame. Divorce has become the other scarlet letter. Shame can be the voice of your abuser or your own thoughts. Guy often mockingly said, "You won't divorce me. It will mean you failed . . . and you can't fail." It freaked me out that Guy knew what I'd been thinking but had never said out loud to him or anyone else. I wouldn't admit what he said was true. I didn't need to.

I already knew I was a failure; my marriage was proof of that. When I did think about it, the words *God hates divorce* reminded me I was stuck in the marriage covenant. There tends to be a stigma in Christianity about divorce; it implies there is something wrong with the woman who couldn't keep her man happy.

If he cheats, she must not like sex. If he hits her, she must have provoked him. If he treats her badly, she must have failed. If he implies she is inferior, then she must be a terrible wife. She is shamed into trying harder, striving to be a better wife, forgiving him for cheating because God hates divorce.

Shame says no matter what you do or don't do, it's your fault. You'll never be enough, but try harder anyway. Fear uses shame to keep you quiet, to keep the family secret. You must not tell, and no one will believe if you do tell. You'll only make it worse. Shame makes you feel alone, as if you are crazy, and that this life is normal . . . so quit complaining.

WHEN GOD DROPS REVELATION ON YOU

In Matthew 5:32, Jesus was asked about divorce. Keep in mind women had no voice, they were considered property, and they couldn't initiate a divorce. Men could cheat all they wanted, but women could not. We know from Malachi 2:13–16, men were kicking their wives out for no reason, heaping violence on them by throwing them out without divorcing them. The women were technically still married, which is why Jesus said marrying them would be adultery. We know God didn't like what the men were doing. He said he hates divorce because of how men treated their wives, the bone of their bone.

That is enough to pause for a moment. We know Jesus treated women, even the "really bad" women, with gentleness, love, and kindness. He called out their sin, yet he also told them to sin no more and that they were healed and whole.

But the verses above sound like women are held to a higher standard than men. I'm not saying I'm right and everyone else is wrong. I'm saying maybe we aren't looking at the whole picture and are assuming some things we shouldn't.

I was in Colorado Springs at my first writers conference and I'd been writing only a couple of years. I was overwhelmed by meeting some of my favorite authors like Liz Curtis Higgs and Jerry Jenkins, and interacting with publishers and agents. I thought I was ready to tell my story, but I wasn't. Shame covered me like an itchy wool blanket. One person asked me, "What's your story?" I had no desire to tell her when God dropped into my mind the words: "I discovered that God loves me more than he hates divorce."

I looked around to see who said it, and yep, it was me. I was more surprised than the person to whom I said it. The realization of how true the statement is set me on a new course. Love trumps hate. Every day, all day. As believers, we've shamed people for divorce without knowing the circumstances that led them to that point.

I'm not an advocate of divorce, and I'm not going to debate whether divorce is right or wrong in your specific case or anyone else's. What I do know is the shame of divorce has kept too many women trapped in horrific marriages. I pursued a divorce Guy didn't want. Since I moved to a new state, I had to wait six months to file. The moment my six months were up, I called my attorney and began the process. A few days before I was going to court to finalize the divorce, I was overwhelmed with shame and dread.

As much as I wanted out of the marriage, I believed God was angry with me. Yet I was willing to risk his anger in order to be free. My dear friend Cindy Smith knew I struggled with getting a divorce, feeling as though I was betraying God. Cindy hugged me and prayed over me. God filled me with a peace I wouldn't understand for a few years. How grateful I was that he sent my friend when I desperately needed her.

For you it may be different—perhaps *he* wanted the divorce. Maybe he tossed you aside like yesterday's garbage, putting all the blame on you for the failed marriage. He spun a tale to all your friends with his side of the story. "She's the problem and won't work on our marriage. I just can't take her craziness any longer. She needs fixing. Look at me, I have it all together. I'm the stable one. I tried, and I just can't do it."

Maybe he planned for that moment, gaslighting you into believing it was all your fault. He might have claimed you were the crazy one, full of anxiety, fear, and shame. He made his case and you lost. Not just yourself, but family and friends. Even the pastor and lay leaders of the church may have believed his story of woe and all he endured for the sake of the kids. It was all an illusion. Yet you may have felt you were the one trapped by shame.

BeLoved, you didn't fail. It's not your fault. God saw you, and one day your abuser will be exposed. God hates abuse more than he hates divorce, and he loves you extravagantly. Allow your heavenly Father to wipe away the shame and blame others have put on you. You are brave and unflinching. No matter what is thrown at you, stand firm in the belief that God is standing with you and will reveal the truth. It's possible those who condemned you will one day apologize for not believing you.

> God hates abuse more than he hates divorce, and he loves you extravagantly.

THE STORY OF GOMER

Gomer's story is told in the book of Hosea. God told Hosea to choose Gomer as his wife because she was unfaithful. God wanted to illustrate to Israel how his people were unfaithful to him. Hosea married Gomer, and they had three children. In her shame, Gomer ran from Hosea and sold herself to other men. She didn't know God watched over her and provided for her. She suffered the consequences of her choices, but he promised to call her back from her pain and shame. He would coax her back to him and lead her into the desert to roll off her shame and leave slavery behind. God promised to restore what was stolen from her and even what she gave away.

In Hosea 2:14–16, God explained through the prophet:

> "But then I will win her back once again.
>   I will lead her into the desert
>   and speak tenderly to her there.
> I will return her vineyards to her
>   and transform the Valley of Trouble into a gateway of hope.
> She will give herself to me there,
>   as she did long ago when she was young,
>   when I freed her from her captivity in Egypt.
> When that day comes," says the LORD,
> "you will call me 'my husband'
> instead of 'my master.'"

God is calling you, dear one, out of your valley of trouble. He's opened the door to healing for you to walk through into hope. Your life will not be defined by what was done to you, but by what *God does* with what was done to you.

I remember being horrified that my story would be my shame as an abused woman. But no. When I surrendered, God freed me from the bondage of my Egypt. Remember all he did to rescue Israel from her abusers, taking her through the wilderness, rolling off her shame and slavery, eventually allowing her to enter the promised land.

The story in Hosea continues in verses 17–18 as God revealed how he will wipe away the impact of your past and give you a future:

> O Israel, I will wipe the many names of Baal from
>   your lips,
>   and you will never mention them again.
> On that day I will make a covenant
>   with all the wild animals and the birds of the sky

and the animals that scurry along the ground
  so they will not harm you.
I will remove all weapons of war from the land,
  all swords and bows,
so you can live unafraid
  in peace and safety.

You may not be able to imagine peace and safety, but it will come as you live like a much-loved bride such as verses 19–20 reveal:

I will make you my wife forever,
  showing you righteousness and justice,
  unfailing love and compassion.
I will be faithful to you and make you mine,
  and you will finally know me as the LORD.

ENCOUNTER GOD

BeLoved, shame has controlled you long enough. Ask me to reveal where shame is hiding and then release the shame to me. Shame no longer has a place in your life, and you will no longer live in disgrace or in your sorrow. I will call you back from your grief when it's time. I am your redeemer, and I will be your husband.

–Jesus
(Isaiah 54:4–6)

REACHING FOR MORE

Your husband covered you in shame, humiliating you to keep you under his control. Satan, your enemy, continues to lie to you to keep you covered in shame. It's time to break free of shame so that you can begin living out loud—audacious and bold!

1. Identify and list the look, the feel, the sound, and the behavior of shame in your life.
2. Identify and list out the lies tied to the look, feel, sound, and behavior of shame.
3. Ask Jesus to show you the truth about each of the lies and write them out.
4. Release your shame to Jesus: Jesus, you said in your Word that you open prison doors and set captives free. I ask you to open the prison door of my heart and release all the shame I've been carrying, shame that isn't mine to carry . . . releasing, releasing, flowing, flowing. Jesus you bore all my pain, shame, and sorrow . . . releasing, releasing, flowing. (Repeat until you feel the shame is gone; picture all the shame going to Jesus.)
5. Write out what you experienced as you released shame to Jesus.

CHAPTER 9

UNFLINCHING

Develop Courage in the Face of Fear

For God has not given us a spirit of fear and timidity, but of power, love, and self-discipline.
—2 Timothy 1:7

Such love has no fear, because perfect love expels all fear.
—1 John 4:18

You know that tingling feeling you get as the hair on the back of your neck rises? Something is off. You feel it in your bones, but you just can't put words to what *it* is. This natural fear protects you from the unseen and unknown. It warns you danger is near and to be on guard.

But what if the danger lives in your home and sleeps in your bed? That is the kind of fear that is embedded in your soul, runs through your veins, pumps into your heart, and brings death to your soul, death to love. The fear meant to protect you turns into terror and endangers you. It's intense and powerful enough to destroy your power, eradicate love from your life, and jumble your brain.

Intense trauma causes you to either fight, flee, or freeze. The abuser uses time and conditioning to remove your ability to fight or flee. Through his tactics of terror, you freeze and appease him, yielding your soul to satisfy his wants, needs, and desires until terror becomes a way of life.

This terror produces a belief that escape is impossible and death is inevitable. This belief keeps you trapped in the cycle of terror as he whispers, "I love you."

Fear is the root of shame and pride that we talked about in the previous chapter and must be dealt with before you can move on. Fear isn't the boss of you. It's neither a friend nor a protector. It is a powerful tool in the hands of the enemy and the abuser.

An abusive husband would have you believe fear is more powerful than love. But the opposite is true. Perfect love hurls fear into the abyss. Imagine Superman throwing a baseball into space, never to see it fall back to earth. That's how perfect love handles fear. One day fear becomes a way of life, though you may not remember the day fear crept in and stole your life and became your normal. Fear has become so much a part of who you are that if it leaves you'll be left with a gaping hole.

Several years ago, I heard a teaching on 2 Timothy 1:7. It answered my biggest *why I stayed* question. I've already told you the multitude of reasons I stayed in the marriage. This verse was the key to unlock all the whys: "For God has not given us a spirit of fear and timidity, but of power, love, and self-discipline." The word *given* in the Greek also means *gift*. God has not *gifted* you with fear or timidity. He has *gifted* you with power, love, and a sound mind.

> **Fear and faith are complete opposites; the enemy uses fear to keep us from faith.**

WHEN FEAR COMES KNOCKING

Fear is an extreme emotion that alerts you of imminent danger, evil, or pain—the threat can be real or imagined, based on what we see or can't see. On the other hand, faith is confidence or trust, a belief not based on proof even when what we see makes no sense. Fear and faith are complete opposites; the enemy uses fear to keep us from faith.

Fear is real when you are required to send your kids to your abusive ex-husband or you lost custody of your children to him. Fear is when no one believes you and the court system sides with him and you're considered the crazy one as he continues to torment you even after the divorce is final.

The abuse may have escalated to the point that you realized you were done, yet circumstances beyond your control trapped you in a house of horrors with no way to escape. You may *still* be recovering as fear whispers, "You're mine—you'll never be free of me."

"When calamity comes knocking on their door, suddenly and without warning they're undone—broken to bits, shattered, with no hope of healing" (Proverbs 6:15 TPT). BeLoved, calamity wants to keep your eyes on the terror surrounding you and not on Jesus.

> BeLoved, calamity wants to keep your eyes on the terror surrounding you and not on Jesus.

During one of our country's economic depressions, I battled fear of losing everything—my health, our home, our business—until I was tied in knots and swirling in chaos. A friend said this: "The enemy will annihilate your hope if he can't kill you." The father of lies was well on his way to burning my hope to ash. But then the Lord stepped into my chaos to remind me of all I've survived: a thirty-year violent marriage, infidelity, abandonment, bankruptcy, and more. Though you were broken, shattered, and hopeless, open your heart to love, to be overcome by Jesus instead of being overcome by fear.

How do you unfasten your eyes from the awful in your life that causes you to spiral into fear and hopelessness and begin to focus your eyes onto Jesus? "We look away from the natural realm and we focus our attention and expectation onto Jesus who birthed faith within us and who leads us forward into faith's perfection. His example is this: Because his heart was focused on the joy of knowing that you would be his, he endured the agony of the cross and conquered its humiliation, and now sits exalted at the right hand of the throne of God!" (Hebrews 12:2 TPT).

Imagine yourself trapped in a burning building. You're on the ledge, you can't go back, and your only option is to jump. Paralyzed by fear, the sounds of chaos, and the searing heat, you finally hear the firefighter. As you turn your eyes to his, he yells, "Look at me, don't look down or back, just look at me." Your only hope if you want to live is to listen to the firefighter's words, keep your eyes locked on his, tune out the sights and sounds of chaos, trust him, and do only what he tells you to do. He's done this hundreds of times, spent hours upon hours training for just this moment.

Even though you can't see Jesus, you can picture him in your mind. Do you want to live? Then look away from the sights and sounds of calamity and fasten your gaze on Jesus. Going back isn't an option. Living in the fire of fear will kill you, both figuratively and literally.

As I write, tears drop from my eyes as I picture Jesus. He and I are forehead to forehead, my eyes locked on his, and I feel his closeness. I'm overcome by his comfort, and I'm strengthened with his peace. When I think of all the struggles and dark corners of the past decade, hopelessness fades into the flames, and I'm washed by the river of his love.

BeLoved, God will do the same for you. It's risky when you feel God is distant, but remember the story of the woman who risked it all to be healed by touching Jesus's robe. Her example will take your eyes off the source of fear and help you lock eyes with Jesus. I'm not saying it's easy, and it seems counterintuitive to ignore the fear that chaos creates, which often feels real and touchable. Yet Scripture comforts us when we focus on Jesus.

Psalm 26:3 tells us that his loving-kindness is right in front of us, and we have walked in God's truth. Loving-kindness in the Hebrew means so much more than we may think; it's mercy, compassion, goodness, unfailing and steadfast love. This is what we keep before our eyes, not fear, not our circumstances, not our abuser.

God's love is deeper, wider, higher than you can imagine. It's not flaky and self-seeking, like your abuser. God's love is the foundation you stand upon. His love is your force field against fear. In other words, when you keep your eyes on Jesus, his perfect love drives fear out of your life so you can live unflinching, resolute, and undaunted.

I make it sound easy, and in a way, it is and isn't. This is the place where you discover courage. It takes courage to face fear. It takes courage to unflinchingly use God's gifts of power, love, and self-discipline. But these are things God has gifted to you. Are you ready to take them back?

TAKE BACK YOUR POWER

Power is the ability to do or act. It is the capacity of doing or accomplishing something. Review the list below, see the authenticity of who you are versus the counterfeit person your husband convinced you you were. Your abuser systematically dismantled your confidence, your potential, and your strength until you felt weak and useless.

Authentic Power	Counterfeit Power
Capable	Impotent
Skilled	Unable
Competent	Incompetent
Talented	Weak
Qualified	Inept
Virtuous	Blameworthy
Strong	Impaired
Mighty	Lacking
Assertive	Subservient
Righteous	Inferior

When your power is gone, you become incompetent, unable to process your thoughts or exert your own will. You begin to like what he likes. For example, Guy liked his steak well-done. I liked my steak medium. I don't know when I changed, but I started ordering my steak well-done. This is a small change, yet it's an example of all the places where I shifted from being me to becoming an extension of him. I gave up my power to choose in order to accept what he wanted.

BeLoved, I realize you may not know *when* you gave up your power and instead became an extension of him. Yet it's time to take back your power, your ability to choose, and become the competent, talented, and qualified woman God created you to be. Then you can discover who you are separate from your husband and stop parroting him.

What food do you like? How do you like your steak? What

toppings do you want on your pizza? What movies do you want to watch? What pleases you? What are your gifts and talents?

What are you capable of? What are your dreams? What do you have to say? What are your views on God, politics, or the weather?

You can take back your power by becoming the woman God created you to be. If you don't know who you are, ask Jesus to show you what you're capable of. Ask him to reveal forgotten dreams, to reveal the authentic you. Read Ephesians chapters 1 through 3 to discover all you are in Jesus. Read these declarations over yourself, write them on your mirror, say them out loud with confidence until you own them:

> Abba/Daddy/Father God (whichever you're the most comfortable with) . . .
> - I am wanted and chosen by you (Ephesians 1:4).
> - I am created and designed by you (Ephesians 2:10).
> - I am secure in your unconditional love (Ephesians 3:14–19).
> - I am the greatest idea you ever had (Genesis 1:26–31). [Say that one again.]
> - I am your masterpiece, your poem, your symphony (Ephesians 2:10).
> - I am confident in your embrace with no fear of rejection (Romans 8:1).
> - You complete the deepest longings of my heart (Hebrews 10:23).
> - I choose to live astonished, astounded, and awed by how you think about me (Psalm 139:14).

TAKE BACK YOUR LOVE

Agape is the purest form of love. It is the sacrificial love God has for us. The greatest commandment we're given is to love God with all our heart, soul, and mind, and love our neighbor as ourselves (Luke 10:27). Love is tender, passionate, and deep affection; it's a warm personal attachment, benevolence, and goodwill.

Is that how you would describe your husband's love for you? Is it honestly still how you feel about him? Have you thought—or whispered—the words, *But I love him*? Do you feel if you stopped saying the words you'd have to admit the truth you're avoiding? How did you feel when your husband spoke loving words to you? Was he tender, passionate, and warm? Did he honor and treasure you?

We are to love as we love ourselves. But abusers have a deep well of self-loathing. Can you see it? How could he love you with agape love? Abusers give the illusion of love to get what they want from you. What he wanted was your devotion, respect, and admiration while he selfishly neglected and despised you, which is evident by his actions. Each time he said, "I love you," he meant, "I despise you. I'll give you my version of love to get what I want from you."

Breathe. I know that sounds harsh and terribly hard to hear. You may have thought the hard part was leaving the abuse. The hardest part is learning what happened to you and deconstructing all you learned from abuse.

Now that I've experienced God's extravagant love, I don't think I ever experienced love from Guy. The most difficult words to say are, "I'm not sure I ever loved Guy." I was enamored by his pursuit of me and thought it meant he loved me. But he couldn't give what he didn't have. When your husband said "I love you," how did it make you feel, based on the words below?

Authentic Love	Counterfeit Love
Affectionate	Antagonized
Appreciated	Disliked
Devoted	Uncaring
Companionable	Hated
Respected	Indifferent
Tender	Neglected
Delightful	Miserable
Cherished	Sorrowful
Treasured	Betrayed

Authentic Love	Counterfeit Love
Embraced	Despised
Admired	Degraded
Faithful	Humiliated
Esteemed	Mocked
Adored	Scorned

BeLoved, I know this is hard to face as it seeps into your soul that though you vowed words of love at your wedding, your husband's definition of love was far different than yours. Devastation may hit as you realize your marriage may have been based on deception and not covenant.

A covenant is a binding oath, a promise. It requires binding action from both parties. It's what marriage should look like, but what if it doesn't? What if he went into your marriage not expecting to make a covenant with you but thinking of something else entirely? He didn't mean his vows, or they represented something completely different to him, though to you it was covenant.

The abuser breaks the marriage covenant by despising you; he cares nothing for the promise he made in the ceremony; he expresses his loathing for you, spurns you, and makes sure you diminsh as he becomes the center of attention. He doesn't see you as valued, nor will he consider what you think. You'll be in a constant state of sorrow, dried up, parched of love and care. Over time he will break your will. With every decision you make, he will question your choices until you don't trust any decision you make. He will shame you, keep you in a constant state of confusion until your life will feel like a wasteland, incapable of sustaining life. He will strip you of everything you value, he'll strip you of your dignity through humiliation, completely isolate you until you struggle to attach to your own children.

You aren't wrong for leaving him. This isn't how a bridegroom treats his bride. You didn't break the marriage covenant by filing for divorce. As I mentioned earlier, he broke it the moment he chose to be an abuser. You may be told you don't have biblical grounds for divorce. But what if you do?

Even though it's been over sixteen years since I left my marriage, I feel the pain of seeing in black and white that Guy didn't love me, couldn't love me. How do you feel as you read this? Surrender the pain of wasted years to Jesus and rejoice that now you can experience authentic love.

> Love speaks words of affirmation, builds you up, sacrifices all for you.

How do you take back love? By recognizing that your views of God and yourself have been skewed by your abuser's twisted view of love. Love isn't a dirty word. Love is pure, intimate, and honorable. It's a commitment to a relationship. Love speaks words of affirmation, builds you up, sacrifices all for you.

Are you willing to open yourself up to God's unbounding love? God loves you with perfect and unique love. Ask him what he loves about you. Listen to what he says, and don't discount it even if it sounds silly to you. His response will never condemn or belittle you.

TAKE BACK YOUR SOUND MIND

Depending on the version of the Bible you're reading, a variety of words are used for "sound mind" to show how multifaceted this word is in Greek. The word means self-discipline, sound judgment, to act sensibly, and be wise. It's having the power to discern and judge what is right or true. Fear scrambles your brain and makes it impossible to act wisely or sensibly. Review the contrast of meanings for wisdom. How did your husband treat you using the words below?

Authentic Sound Mind	Counterfeit Sound Mind
Astute	Careless
Aware	Foolish
Careful	Heedless
Enlightened	Idiotic
Informed	Ignorant
Judicious	Insensitive
Knowledgeable	Irrational
Perceptive	Reckless

Authentic Sound Mind	Counterfeit Sound Mind
Prudent	Stupid
Rational	Thoughtless
Sane	Unaware
Sensible	Uninformed
Wary	Unintelligent
Contemplative	Unknowledgeable
Smart	Unrealistic
Sage	Unreasonable
Sound	Unsound
Discerning	Unwise
Intuitive	Dull

The book of Proverbs tells us to seek wisdom as if we are on a treasure hunt. We are to cry out for understanding and insight, to tune our ears for wisdom. God is the one who gives wisdom. Abuse distorts our ability to hear God clearly and twists wisdom to the point that we doubt every choice we make. We begin looking to our husband for what we should do rather than looking to God. That was your abuser's goal: to turn you from authentic truth to his counterfeit version of truth. We become double-minded to the point of constantly changing our minds, which leaves us feeling unsettled.

Your husband kept you in a state of confusion and indecision by attacking your ability to choose. He asked you to choose an option, but then he'd override you until you lost all confidence to make the right choice. Over time you became paralyzed when a decision needed to be made. No wonder it was hard to leave: you couldn't trust yourself to choose wisely. He used fear to keep you unbalanced and unstable.

God will give you clarity as you pursue wisdom and reclaim your power to choose. Give yourself grace as you heal and struggle to make decisions, whether they are right or wrong. You'll regain your sound mind and grow confident as you choose to heal. It will get easier, though it may not help when it comes to deciding where you want to go for dinner.

THE UGLY TRUTH ABOUT FEAR

Fear and timidity come from the whispered lies of Satan to keep you from living the life God intends for you. God gifts you with power, love, and a sound mind.

Living with an abuser keeps you in a constant state of powerlessness and makes you unable to act, even if you could create a plan to leave.

Fear isn't compatible with love. It's like attempting to put the north ends of two magnets together. As you push them closer, you can feel the resistance. The magnets push apart because their forces aren't compatible. What we think is love isn't. Fear makes it difficult to love our children or ourselves. It makes it difficult to attach or feel tenderness. An abuser isolates his victim so she feels unloved by her family and friends, and eventually he becomes her only source for love.

Fear confuses sound judgment and wisdom to where you are unable to recognize what's right or true. Through the tactic of gaslighting, he's conditioned you to doubt everything you know and understand so you'll act irrational, feel foolish, stupid, and unreasonable.

Love is our greatest weapon against fear. Perfect love expels *all* fear (1 John 4:18). Fear cannot stand in the face of love, because love involves sacrifice. "This is real love—not that we loved God, but that he loved us and sent his Son as a sacrifice to take away our sins" (verse 10).

Jesus is love and our example for love. We're to love like him. We're to be immersed in his love. You may not be able to wrap your mind around this concept just yet, but you will.

ENCOUNTER GOD

BeLoved, find a quiet place, close your eyes, and ask me to come close—forehead to forehead. Sit for a moment, don't rush. Engage your senses and focus on me. Ignore the sounds around you. Breathe in and let your breath out slowly. Feel my presence, my overwhelming peace, and the complete lack of fear.

-Jesus
(James 4:7)

REACHING FOR MORE

Fear can be good; it's designed to warn you of danger. The fear that is imbedded in your soul from abuse is crippling and polarizing. It's fear designed to take your power, love, and sound mind. You may feel as though you're anything but courageous—today is a new day brave girl! You can stand unflinching in the face of fear.

1. Create "I am" statements you can read every day to show how you are regaining your power.
2. Create "I am" statements you can read every day to show how you are reclaiming love.
3. Create "I am" statements you can read every day to show how you are reengaging your sound mind.
4. What will you do when fear comes knocking on your door? Hint: Don't answer. Kick it to the curb. (Come up with your own cliché to knock the teeth out of fear.)
5. Ask Jesus how he sees you. Ask him what he likes about you. Ask him who he created you to be. Write it out, read it, then say it out loud. Thank him. Praise him. If you can't find the words, read Psalm 139.

PART 4

CONQUEROR
Living Undaunted

A re you ready to crush the father of lies? To be so close to Jesus that when Satan comes knocking you say, "Whatever"? Are you ready to take back territory that was stolen from you and step out of your past and seize your future?

It's time to begin new, leave old behind, and become all God created you to be. You can wipe away the residue of abuse and know beyond a shadow of doubt that you are loved as you were meant to be loved.

You are his delight, the apple of his eye, his BeLoved one. You are the one he sacrificed his Son for. You'll no longer be known as not loved, not belonging, not seen, and not enough.

Instead, you'll know you are loved, You are his, you are worthy, seen, and watched over. You are more than enough.

"For God has made us to be more than conquerors, and his demonstrated love is our glorious victory over everything!" (Romans 8:37 TPT).

CHAPTER 10

UNSHACKLED

Live Freely and Fully

O Lord, you are so good, so ready to forgive, so full of unfailing love for all who ask for your help.
—Psalm 86:5

I would have despaired unless I had believed that I would see the goodness of the LORD in the land of the living.
—Psalm 27:13 (NASB)

Living unshackled after being in bondage for so long can feel like riding in an out-of-control car rushing headlong into a brick wall without hitting the brakes. It also means living in a way that is unsurpassed and unbeatable. Wouldn't you love to surpass where you've been and become unbeatable? Oh, to live determined, fierce, and adamant!

Your husband may have used most of his energy to break your spirit, and to take the fight out of you so he could contain you in his box. The last thing you need is to be physically free and emotionally still ramming into the walls of your abuser's box.

My hope is that, as you're reading, you catch a glimpse of God's heart for you because you may very well need to cling to those promises as we talk about forgiveness.

Before you panic, we'll talk about what forgiveness isn't and what it is. At this point forgiveness may feel like a swear word to you. That's understandable, but see how you feel after I've had a chance to explain what this word really means and the impact forgiveness can have on your future.

A woman who sees her value and loves herself has no room for bitterness or revenge.

When you forgive someone, you're acting upon your strength as a woman of valor, a woman who has learned how to love well. A woman who sees her value and loves herself has no room for bitterness or revenge. Besides, the best way to repay the one who hurt you is to become healed and whole and to forgive. Forgiveness is the opposite of revenge.

THE BEGINNING OF HEALING

Forgiving can feel like giving your abuser a free pass and allowing him to be free of consequences. But that is not the case. I understand if you may want him to suffer as you've suffered. I did. Yet the Scriptures remind us in Romans 12:19 to leave revenge to God: "'Vengeance is mine, I will repay,' says the Lord" (NASB). Our God is more in the business of redemption than revenge. And again, I understand if it doesn't feel right that you have to live with what the abuser did to you.

About a month after I left the marriage, I heard Guy "got right with Jesus" *again*. I was beyond angry—especially when my pastor expected me to come home and support Guy in his decision. As if coming to Jesus set the world right. Guy said he was sorry, so I was to forgive and forget thirty years of abuse and stand by my man? I felt those instructions meant I didn't matter, that what he did to his family was dismissed as trivial. The betrayal was deep. Even now I can't seem to find words to describe what happened to my heart in that moment.

Normally I would rejoice when someone returned to Jesus, but this felt like manipulation, not on the part of my pastor, who only knew what Guy told him, but from Guy. That tactic worked a year and a half earlier, why not again? I also felt betrayed by God. He welcomed Guy back into the fold, and now I should forgive and forget all Guy did?

A few months after I left the marriage, I thought I had to forgive Guy in order to please Jesus. It seemed easy, too easy. It was because I ignored the pain and pretended to be strong. Several years later, when I went through a thirteen-week group focused on healing from abuse and trauma, it became evident as I processed the trauma for the first time that I hadn't forgiven Guy at all.

I allowed myself to talk about the pain, letting the anger flow, telling myself forgiveness is at the end of the book. I dreaded the last chapter, yet as I sat in my home office, I imagined Guy sitting across from me. I let him *have it*, I held nothing back as I poured out my pain and then released and forgave him. I no longer wanted to hold on to bitterness and revenge or give him access to my life. Yes, up to this point I wanted revenge. I wanted Guy to suffer. Hearing how his extended family surrounded him and took him to church was frustrating. As if he was fragile and broken because his wife left him.

This is another ugly side of abuse: As victims, we live with the pain the abuser caused, while the abuser goes on his merry way, seemingly without a care in the world. I still live with the consequences of Guy's abuse, just like you live with the consequences of what your abuser did to you. It just doesn't seem fair.

> My healing began with an understanding of what forgiveness isn't.

But then again, who ever said life was fair? That reasoning made the thought of forgiveness beyond difficult.

I may sound bitter. At the time I was. I hadn't processed what I survived or any of the emotions or pain. I was still numb and in shock and had a long way to go toward healing. But my healing began with an understanding of what forgiveness isn't.

WHAT FORGIVENESS IS NOT

Forgiveness does not mean dismissing pain from your mind. It isn't acting as if the abuse, pain, and betrayal never happened. I've heard people say, "Just forgive and forget" as if that's even possible, especially when your dreams are haunted by memories, humiliation, and pain. You wake with the residue of nightmares that haunt you throughout your day, jumping at every sound, seeing monsters in the closet. Forgiveness isn't forgetting; it's remembering without trauma and pain. In fact, Scripture never uses the phrase "forgive and forget" except in relation to God forgetting our sins (see Psalm 103:8–12).

Forgiveness is not wiping the slate clean. You're not letting him off the hook or excusing his behavior. There isn't an excuse big enough. Yes, we know that hurt people hurt people, but that implies they couldn't help themselves or they are a product of their childhood. Their father was an abuser so they became one too. That is false. No matter what happened to any of us in our past, we are still responsible for our choices as adults. Forgiveness isn't excusing the abuse. In Colossians 3:5–9, Paul tells abusers to stop their abusive behavior. God doesn't excuse bad behavior; rather, he tells us to stop it.

Forgiveness is not kissing and making up just so they can do it again. Perhaps you've done that, and they became more ruthless. Forgiveness isn't appeasing.

First Samuel 18 tells the story of David and Saul's tumultuous relationship: Saul kept a jealous eye on David. David played the harp to soothe Saul's chaotic soul, and Saul suddenly picked up a spear and threw it, attempting to pin David to the wall. Twice. David escaped. When those attempts at murder didn't work, Saul sent him to battle so David would be killed.

In chapter 19 Saul ordered David to be assassinated since he didn't die in battle. After all that, David went back to serve Saul, and yet again Saul tried to kill him. The remainder of 1 Samuel tells the story of Saul hunting David. No matter what David did to appease Saul, the abuse escalated. They never kissed and made up.

Forgiveness does not mean letting bygones be bygones. You don't have to go back to your husband or allow him access or the ability to cross your boundaries. Forgiveness isn't always reconciling. In the story of David and Saul, they never reconciled. Not because of David but due to Saul, who never turned back to God. He died hating David (1 Samuel 31).

Forgiveness does not mean turning the other cheek. You can't forgive until you process the pain. It's like putting a bandage on a broken leg. Forgiveness isn't ignoring the pain and allowing him to abuse you again and again. "But God didn't let Saul find [David]" (1 Samuel 23:14). David and Saul never reconciled.

Forgiveness does not mean letting them off easy. It may seem as if they don't suffer consequences; it's as if they are a nonstick pan and everything slides off them. The truth is they don't care about consequences. To abusers, consequences are bumps in the road. They think they are persecuted, ever the victim. Forgiveness isn't removing the consequences. When Saul encountered Jesus in Acts 9, he was radically saved, but Acts 9:13 and 26 reveal the church was still afraid of Saul, now Paul. Though he changed, the consequences of his actions didn't immediately end. Paul took his time proving he was no longer the man he had been, and it's clear from Scripture he wasn't offended that they didn't trust him.

Forgiveness doesn't mean giving him power. It's the opposite. He loses his ability to control and manipulate you. Forgiveness doesn't give him more power over you; it takes away his power to control you. From the story of David and Saul in 1 Samuel, David was careful to stay far away from Saul and not give Saul access to harm him yet again.

WHAT FORGIVENESS IS

Forgiveness releases you from the bondage of the enemy and your abuser. Satan can shout his accusations at you, but they have no power. You're released from pain; it no longer controls you. It opens you to intimacy, to be known, not just by others but by God.

Forgiveness delivers you from the judgments of the father of lies and your abuser.

Forgiveness redeems your past. Jesus paid a steep price so you could live freely. You can be liberated from the past, from mistakes you made, and from all that's been done to you. You can have victory.

TO FORGIVE OR NOT

Forgiveness in the Greek means to leave or abandon, or to pardon. *Pardon* doesn't mean they aren't guilty or that they didn't harm you. It means you release them from your retribution and leave them to God. Is it easy? Some say yes, it's an act of our will. I say it's hard, and it should be.

I questioned why God would ask me to forgive Guy. After all, I'm not God. It seems only he has the ability to forgive. Why would he ask us to do the impossible?

Jesus responded to Peter's question about forgiveness in Matthew 18 with a parable. I've struggled with this parable, mostly because I didn't understand it—especially verse 35 when Jesus said: "That's what my heavenly Father will do to you if you refuse to forgive your brothers and sisters from your heart." It sounds harsh and condemning, which doesn't sound like Jesus and how he responded to the people he interacted with. He healed them, forgave their sins, and had compassion on them.

What if I'm hearing it wrong? What if I missed the point and assigned meaning what wasn't there? A dear friend used this passage to teach about forgiveness. She said if we truly understood the depth of forgiveness, we would live differently. I'm still pondering that thought. I thought I did grasp Jesus's forgiveness, but her statement had me rethinking what I believe about forgiveness.

How did I not see it before? I couldn't see it because there was still a part of me that believed God isn't always good and has a streak of meanness. With all the evil in the world, it can be easy to come to the wrong conclusion about God. Grab your Bible and read the parable in Matthew 18:21–35 as I share the story in a nutshell.

One day the king decided to go over his books to see who owed him money so he could collect the debts. One name jumped out at him. This man owed him millions, more money than the indebted one could repay. The king ordered the man and his family to be taken into custody, tossed into prison, and to sell off all they owned to repay the debt.

For the man who owed money, one day life was good and the next, everything was gone, his family destitute. When the man was brought before the king, he fell at the feet of the king and begged for mercy, promising to repay all he owed. The heart of the king was moved, and instead of giving the man more time to repay, he forgave the debt altogether. *What?* Just like that his debt of millions was cleared, he could go back to his nice home and belongings, his wife and kids, free from the bondage of debt.

But instead of going home, he went to the home of another man who owed him thousands of dollars and demanded he repay all he owed. Why would he do this? It became clear that he didn't believe the king; he didn't accept the gift of forgiveness and mercy. He repaid good with evil.

The man who owed thousands begged for time to repay all he owed. Instead of showing mercy, the man who was just forgiven a much larger debt tossed the other man and his family in prison. Seriously? When the other servants saw what happened, they were outraged and told the king.

The king sent for the man again, only this time the man who had owed millions got anything but mercy. After berating him, the king tossed the man into prison to be tortured until he paid his original debt of millions. He was never getting out of jail and most likely wished for a speedy death.

Here's where verse 35 comes in. Jesus hadn't yet paid the price for our sins, but he knew it was coming. As he hung on the cross, before the sins of the world were laid on him, he extended forgiveness, "Father, forgive them, for they don't know what they are doing" (Luke 23:34).

Think on that for a moment. Jesus forgave all the people who followed him throughout his ministry, who a week earlier shouted their praise as he entered Jerusalem on Palm Sunday, and then turned on him as he hung on the cross for them. Back to verse 35, if we *refuse* to forgive, we will be tormented. I pondered on this verse, struggling with understanding, when Jesus turned on the light . . . the key is in the word *refuse*. Taking time to process trauma isn't *refusing* to forgive and neither is not being *ready* to forgive.

Most trauma victims need time to understand the dynamics of abuse and come to grips with the facts of what happened and the extent of the abuse throughout the marriage. Not everyone can admit their marriage was abusive; some get stuck in the fantasy of what they thought was a fairy tale. It is a horrifying moment to realize your fairy tale was a nightmare.

Another key of forgiveness is to forgive from your heart. We forgive from our innermost being. Before we can forgive from the inside, we first must face the pain we've stored there. You can't forgive what you don't acknowledge or feel. Again, taking time to acknowledge and process pain is key to forgiving, along with taking time to grieve all you lost, all that was stolen, and all you missed.

There's no doubt forgiving can be difficult and beyond your ability. You have to live with the consequences of the abuser's behavior and not hold him accountable. I said this earlier in the chapter: Is God asking you to do something beyond what you're willing to do? Yes.

Unforgiveness is carrying the weight of another's burdens—a burden only Jesus was meant to carry, a burden he carried on the cross. We've covered how abusers can't or won't carry their own pain, that they put it on others to carry it for them. When we release and forgive our abusers, we put that burden back on Jesus and put our abusers in Jesus's hands.

Some would rather stay a victim and choose to live shackled to unforgiveness and bitterness. From this parable, we know that is a dangerous place to be. It is a place of torment, living in a prison of our own making.

Unforgiveness hinders healing and keeps you a victim as you rehearse all the abuser did to you instead of processing the pain. Unforgiveness keeps you trapped in your past and pain; forgiveness propels you into your future.

Psalm 27:13 promises that you will see God's goodness in the land of the living, where you are revived, where it's safe to return to living—not just trudging through life, but living where God breathes life into you as you release the trauma and the right to seek revenge. When you are ready to release the burden of all your abuser did to you, invite the Holy Spirit to fill up the empty places.

WHAT IF?

What if forgiving is the greatest act of love? "We know what real love is because Jesus gave up his life for us" (1 John 3:16).

What if forgiving means evil is conquered? "Yet even in the midst of all these things, we triumph over them all, for God has made us to be more than conquerors, and his demonstrated love is our glorious victory over everything!" (Romans 8:37 TPT).

What if forgiving gives you back your power? "For God has not given us a spirit of fear and timidity, but of power, love, and self-discipline" (2 Timothy 1:7).

What if forgiving increases your capacity for love, joy, and peace? "But the Holy Spirit produces this kind of fruit in our lives: love, joy, peace, patience, kindness, goodness, faithfulness, gentleness, and self-control" (Galatians 5:22–23).

What if forgiving puts responsibility back on the abuser? "I will tell about your righteous deeds all day long, for everyone who tried to hurt me has been shamed and humiliated" (Psalm 71:24).

What if you could be freer than you've ever been? "Never take revenge. Leave that to the righteous anger of God. For the Scriptures say, 'I will take revenge; I will pay them back,' says the LORD" (Romans 12:19).

You can overcome by heeding Romans 12:21: "Don't let evil conquer you, but conquer evil by doing good."

You survived evil, not the boogeyman you hear about in the news or watch in movies, but one who lived in your house, slept in your bed, and fooled the world. There is a greater evil in the world—one who wants to kill, steal, and destroy you (John 10:10). According to 1 John 5:19, "the world around us is under the control of the evil one."

We can conquer evil with good. How can we do that? Forgiveness provides you the opportunity to do good toward the one who hurt you. You still need boundaries, he doesn't get free rein in your life, you don't have to trust him, but you can forgive and release him to God. I'm telling you it will drive him absolutely mad that he can no longer control, manipulate, or gaslight you. You'll see his tactics, and one day you may even feel pity for him.

> When you choose a life of healing and forgiveness, you live an excellent, fine, and quality life.

The word *good* in the Greek means excellent, fine, quality. Let me put it this way: When you choose a life of healing and forgiveness, you live an excellent, fine, and quality life. Now isn't that better than revenge? Walking in freedom and wholeness so the abuse no longer has power over you? Where you stop revolving around his world?

The biggest secret about forgiveness is that it has very little to do with the people who hurt you. Forgiveness has everything to do with you and how much you are loved. God provides a way for you to break out of jail and live a life of freedom despite your circumstances.

One day you may even get to the place Job did, where he could pray for those who maligned him and God: "When Job prayed for his friends, the Lord restored his fortunes" (Job 42:10). According to verse 7, Job's friends spoke inaccurately about who God is.

ENCOUNTER GOD

Treasured one, allow yourself to grieve as I did in the garden of Gethsemane. As a man about to die, I grieved what was coming so you would know that I know how agonizing grief is. Most of your friends will not understand and may not have the capacity to grieve with you. You may feel alone, but you aren't. Lean into my presence by coming into our secret place. I will comfort you as you pour out your heart. When you are ready, choose to forgive those who hurt you and release yourself to live freely for my glory. I can't wait to show you how.

-The one who has always loved you, Jesus
(Matthew 26:36–46; Psalm 91; Luke 23:34)

REACHING FOR MORE

You may not be ready to forgive, not because you won't but because you may not be ready. You may have more healing to do before you can forgive and release your ex-husband. That is okay. Don't rush the process, and don't allow others to tell you when it's time. If you're agreeable, can you respond to a few questions? Be honest with where you are. It's time to unshackle some chains.

1. Before you read this chapter, did you believe you had to forgive or God would be mad at you? How has your thinking shifted?
2. Describe how you feel, knowing that God wants you to face what was done to you before you forgive.
3. Review the statements about what forgiveness isn't, then write out how you feel as you read each one. Is there anything you would add?
4. Review the statements about what forgiveness is, then write out how you feel as you read. Is there anything that surprised you?
5. Go back to the "What If?" section on pages 146–47 and write out each what-if question and one of the Scriptures. Process how you feel and, if you're able, name the emotions that rise up.

CHAPTER 11

UNSHAKABLE

Live Boldly and Bravely

I don't depend on my own strength to accomplish this; however I do have one compelling focus: I forget all of the past as I fasten my heart to the future instead.
—Philippians 3:13 (TPT)

Now listen, daughter, pay attention, and forget about your past. Put behind you every attachment to the familiar, even those who once were close to you!
—Psalm 45:10 (TPT)

The movie *Mortal Engines* has an interesting backstory. The creepy cyborg character Shrike was made of broken things, so he gathered broken toys, machines, and a tender girl, who is scarred inside and out. The girl was broken so he would fix her by making her like him . . . wires and metal. She would no longer remember the pain of what broke her. She would be dead, but living. But the moment she found real love, she escaped from him, and he determined to hunt her down. The broken in Shrike fueled his desire to destroy her. In the end, love healed her memories and pain, and Shrike could not stand against her love.

Just like Shrike, Satan gathers the broken ones, promising to take away their pain through deception, drugs, alcohol, numbness, apathy, or perfection, to name a few. The enemy of your soul will use anything and everything to keep you as the living dead.

Jesus's sacrifice was the greatest act of love. He carried your pain and wounds so you could live fully alive without the burden of shame from painful memories. His love set you free when he rose from the grave and defeated death. You were buried with Jesus, and your past stayed there when he arose, although we tend to dig up the past and carry it around like a trophy.

Wouldn't it be wonderful to break the hold the past has on you? Wouldn't it be amazing to know that our pasts don't have to break our futures?

Humiliation crushed me with every memory. It shouted failure so I dulled the pain by pretending the past didn't matter.

You may ask, "How did that work for you?" It didn't. And it won't work for you either.

Philippians 3:13 instructs us to "focus on this one thing: Forgetting the past and looking forward to what lies ahead." There are three principles you can activate from this verse. Each principle includes your part and God's part. You can't do God's part, and he won't do yours.

1. You can't tough it out, but you can be a woman who *depends* on God's strength.
2. You can't change your past, but you can be a woman who *conquers* her past.
3. You can't envision the future, but you can be a woman who boldly *embraces* the future.

> God doesn't want you to be a strong woman who depends on her own strength to survive; he wants you to be a woman of strength—depending on his strength as you heal.

A WOMAN OF STRENGTH

You can try to tough it out, but you'll end up exhausted and drained of what little strength you do have. God doesn't ask you to tough it out, to suffer alone or on your own. Just because you *can* handle a lot doesn't mean you *should*. God doesn't want you to be a strong woman who depends on her own strength to survive; he wants you to be a woman of strength—depending on his strength as you heal.

You may have felt weak and powerless in your marriage, and now you long to feel strong. Most people who hear about your struggle may see you as weak because you stayed in an abusive marriage. They couldn't be more wrong. They don't understand the conditioning he did to train you to put him above your own needs and the needs of your kids. Besides that, he was sucking you dry of strength, so you'd feel weak and powerless.

Ephesians 6:10 says, "Be strong in the Lord and in his mighty power." *Strong* in the Greek means "to receive strength; be strengthened for service or action; to make someone strong." It's in Jesus that we are strong: We access his power through faith. We can believe him even when we don't understand. We can trust him even when what we see doesn't make sense. And in the mustard seed of our sometimes wavering faith, we can be confident he will keep his promises.

What does it mean to be a woman of strength? How do you stand firm against Satan? According to Ephesians 6:11, you put on God's armor so you can stand firm against the onslaught of the enemy, Satan, who attempts to retraumatize you with memories of your past.

Is it easy? No.

Will you slip? Probably.

Will you get up? Without a doubt.

Isaiah 41:10 instructs: "Don't be afraid, for I am with you. Don't be discouraged, for I am your God. *I will strengthen you and help you.* I will hold you up with my victorious right hand" (emphasis added). The word *strengthen* in Hebrew means "to be stout, strong, bold, and alert."

In God's kingdom, life is the opposite of what we expect. When you want to be strong, you become weak. Weakness can be your natural limitations or bodily weakness from illness or trauma. The Lord says in 2 Corinthians 12:9, "My grace is all you need. My power works best in weakness."

Let me say it this way. God is delighted in you and wants to pour out his kindness, goodwill, favor, and generosity on you because you require relief from trauma and your past. His resurrection power will give you the strength you so desperately need.

You're not in this fight alone. Even Jesus was completely dependent on his Father. Jesus didn't do or say anything without talking to his Father first. Resist the urge to tough it out. Instead, lean on him for your strength. What does it look like to lean on him? Proverbs 3:5–6 holds the key by reminding you to place yourself in his hands. Don't trust in what you think you understand, but talk to God about the pain, the trauma, and the difficulties. He promises to guide you through every part of this journey of healing.

CONQUER YOUR PAST

I find much comfort in this promise: "Who shall separate us from the love of Christ? Shall tribulation, or distress, or persecution, or famine, or nakedness, or danger, or sword? As it is written, 'For your sake we are being killed all the day long; we are regarded as sheep to be slaughtered.' No, in all these things we are more than conquerors through him who loved us" (Romans 8:35–37 ESV).

Here's my paraphrase of verse 35: "Can your abuser separate you from the love of Jesus? Shall severe suffering, great pain, oppression, extreme misery, violence, exposure to injury, or aggression separate you from the love of your Abba Father? *No!* Can your anger, unbelief, and distrust keep you from his love? *No!*"

For thirty years, I thought it did. As I write, tears fill my eyes. I'm overwhelmed that I could ever believe *anything* could keep me from the love of Jesus. You may be feeling similar emotions, or you may still be grappling with what you just read.

Here is fabulous news. Even though you endured all this pain, you can conquer, subdue, vanquish, clobber, and frustrate the evil one by embracing the God who loves you.

According to *The New Strong's Complete Dictionary of Bible Words*, the word *conqueror* means "to have complete triumph, win a most thorough, overwhelming victory, or be triumphantly or overwhelmingly victorious." Scripture states *this* is who you were made to be.

You can't entertain the voice of the evil one and expect to conquer the past. Conquer is a military term; it's aggressive and purposeful. It's not something you do by accident or just fall into. You can't be a passivist in a spiritual battle.

Satan whispers in your ear, reminding you that you're a failure, reminding you of how unworthy you are, that you're just not enough. You think it's your thoughts, or worse, God's thoughts toward you. Not so. It's time to take your thoughts captive, grab them by the throat, and toss them out of your mind by refusing to listen (2 Corinthians 10:5). I sometimes say out loud, "Stop!" I'll remind myself who God truly is and who he says I am. You can do the same by telling yourself that you are a daughter of the King, you are a joint heir with Christ—meaning all that is his is yours, and you are his bride, the apple of his eye, his BeLoved.

> The more time you spend with Jesus, listen to his voice, and read his Word, the more you'll recognize the tactics the father of lies uses to keep you trapped in your past.

This isn't a one and done. It's a way of life. The more time you spend with Jesus, listen to his voice, and read his Word, the more you'll recognize the tactics the father of lies uses to keep you trapped in your past. Remember the fallen one is already defeated; it's the one thing he doesn't want you to know: the war is already won.

BOLDLY EMBRACE YOUR FUTURE

After surrendering to God's strength, and learning how to conquer our past, our next step is to release control and manipulation. You might be thinking, *But I'm not controlling or a manipulator!* Consider this: During your marriage when you were in the "good times," did you find yourself walking on eggshells, attempting to keep him happy, doing what pleased him, catering to him, and keeping the kids quiet only to have all your efforts blow up in your face?

I didn't think I was a controller or manipulator either until one day God dropped a statement in my mind: "It's time to give up manipulation." *What?* "You needed control and manipulation to survive the marriage. You don't need them any longer." His words pierced my heart. What a relief it was to release it all to him. These were two things I didn't want to take into my future.

If you're ready, you can say, "Jesus, I release control and manipulation to you." Go ahead. Say it aloud. You can do it. Now . . . doesn't that feel fabulous?

Only God knows what your future looks like. He may drop hints, but he rarely gives you the full picture.

From where you stand, your future may look bleak and scary. You may not be able to imagine living without pain and grief. You may be living in a continual nightmare as your ex-husband harasses you on a daily basis. Your future may feel like you're driving in dense fog.

Years ago, I started a thirty-mile drive from one small town to another even smaller town. It was foggy, but I could see the cars ahead of me. Once I left town, the fog became so thick I couldn't see beyond the hood of my car or out my side windows. Stopping, pulling over, or turning around was more terrifying than driving blindly forward. I made it to my destination safe, but shaky. Too bad my vehicle didn't come with technology that would keep me in my lane and warn me if other cars were around me. Proverbs 3:6 is our stay-safe-in-emotional-fog technology: "Seek his will in all you do, and he will show you which path to take."

That is what it feels like to step into your future. Instead of driving slowly and steadily, Scripture says to stretch and strain toward the future. The Bible says it this way: "She is clothed with strength and dignity, and she laughs without fear of the future" (Proverbs 31:25). There's a reason she can laugh without fear. We have a God who is personally involved. Who steps from heaven and whispers the course corrections.

When you can't see what's ahead, you make the next right move. Your future is tomorrow, then the next day, and the next. One step at a time. Sounds cliché, yet it doesn't make it any less true. Matthew 6:31–34 reminds us not to worry about what we will eat, drink, or wear but to seek after the kingdom and God will provide all we need. So don't torment yourself with disturbing thoughts about what's in your future.

I'm not saying your future will be easy or without problems. It can be distressful not knowing how you'll provide for yourself and your kids, where you'll live and find a job, and so on. Healing is difficult, pain is hard, grieving is like riding a roller coaster every day.

Moving forward requires trust in God. You may not yet trust him, and that's okay. Trust takes time, and he is okay with you taking that time to learn to trust him. I think the Christian life is all about learning to trust God, as every day stretches our level of trust in him.

You can step into the future with confident expectation and hope, relying on God's strength, his ability to provide for you and protect you, and his integrity to keep the promises in his Word. Sounds like an adventure instead of a life sentence.

After more than sixteen years of healing and growing in Jesus, I wish I could tell you I trust God implicitly. But it seems that each year brings up situations where I learn to trust him on a deeper level. It's part of being a believer, constantly learning new facets of God's character and faithfulness.

WHEN IT'S TIME TO REMEMBER

Do you realize God collects your tears? In Psalm 56:8, David sang: "You keep track of all my sorrows. You have collected all my tears in your bottle. You have recorded each one in your book."

You may think your tears have gone unnoticed, but they haven't. Read the verse again, "You did not lose track of me in my sorrow. You captured my tears in your bottle" (my paraphrase). Do you wonder what God's written in his book about your tears? I do too.

Each tear you shed is recorded in *his* book. To *record* is not just to write something down, but writing for the purpose of *preserving*. God is tracking, collecting, and preserving your sorrow and tears. He does not take your pain lightly, yet he will use your story to bring healing to others. Not today maybe, but one day when you're ready.

The first time I read that God would use my pain to heal others, I felt anger, shame, and fear rise up inside of me. I didn't want anyone to know my story. I didn't want anyone to see inside my secret life and judge me or, worse, pity me.

God wastes nothing and uses everything that was meant to destroy you. The story of Joseph in Genesis 37–50 is a powerful story of a spoiled kid, jealous brothers, envy, lies, abuse, kidnapping, slavery, and redemption. Joseph had dreams and a beautiful coat, was loved by his doting father, and was hated by his ten older brothers.

Life was good for Joseph, until he found himself in a pit he couldn't crawl out of. He must have felt betrayal and confusion when his brothers, who should have loved him, tossed him in a pit and talked of killing him. You may feel emotions stirring inside of you right now. If so, hold on to those emotions for a moment.

Holy Spirit, wrap your precious daughter in your presence as her emotions are stirred.

Joseph didn't die a physical death, but he died a slow emotional death when his brothers sold him off like a bag of grain. He wouldn't forget their faces, ugly and distorted with disgust as they pulled him out of the pit and handed him over to strangers for a bag of money. Frightened, abandoned, betrayed, deceived—what more could go wrong for Joseph?

He was sold off once again, and his life improved as he came under the care of a trusting owner who put him in charge of all the owner had. But then Joseph had to fend off his owner's seductive wife, was accused of rape, and was thrown in prison for a crime he didn't commit. It's clear that at some point Joseph decided to make the best of his circumstances and remain an honorable man.

Hear me. I'm not saying you should have stayed in an abusive marriage.

The amazing part of Joseph's story is that he was eventually freed from prison for interpreting Pharaoh's two dreams and was promoted to second in command of Egypt to oversee the food supply during the coming famine. Through the famine, Joseph came face-to-face with his betrayers when his brothers came to buy food.

If you'll let him, God will use your story of healing to help others.

Eventually, Joseph revealed himself to his brothers. They were terrified he'd seek revenge, but he didn't. When their father died, the brothers were again fearful Joseph would seek revenge. Instead, Joseph said, "You intended to harm me, but God intended it all for good" (Genesis 50:20). His brothers did harm him, but God took those plans for harm and designed a new plan—one for Joseph's benefit, prosperity, and happiness.

God gathered all of Joseph's sorrows, pain, and tears and used them to write a new ending—an ending that was victorious. BeLoved, he is doing the same for you. As I've said before, abuse isn't part of God's plan to make you a better Christian or a better woman, but if you'll let him, God will use your story of healing to help others.

There is a time to remember, not to focus on the trauma but to highlight what God did with your trauma. He's rewriting your past into a new story, using every tear you shed as the ink to preserve your story for your family and future generations.

I will say again, you didn't go through domestic violence so you would have a testimony to share. But God will not waste what was done to you; he'll use your story to help others find the freedom you're walking in.

SHARING YOUR STORY

One day you may want to share your story with others, or you may feel God is calling you to write a book. If the thought of telling your story scares you, then you're not ready and you're not required to share, even if someone asks. It took me years to be able to share my story, and when I do, I rarely go into the gory details. It can be too much for some women and can retraumatize them, which isn't our goal. Make your story mostly about what God is doing with the awful that was done to you.

When I was a young believer, I'd share my testimony of rebellion, drinking, drugs, smoking, and cussing. Then I'd spend five minutes talking about how I came to Jesus. I had it all backward. I made my story about me, not him. I was getting the glory, not God. It revealed my immaturity.

There sometimes exists a compulsion to share our ugly, but our ugly won't help anyone heal, especially if we are unintentionally on a constant one-up with others to see who had it worse. I'm not saying you shouldn't talk about what happened to you. You do need to talk about it, but that doesn't mean you need to tell *everyone*. And it doesn't mean you have to talk about *everything.* Not everyone can handle your story or your pain, and not everyone can handle all your details. It might be too much for them. Find a good trauma counselor and one or two women who can mentor you through your unknown future. They can help you focus on healing from trauma.

Scripture provides a helpful guideline when it comes to telling our stories: "Those who are wise will take all this to heart; they will see in our history the faithful love of the LORD" (Psalm 107:43). This can be the goal when telling your story—to show women what God did in your life so they know he will do the same for them. There will always be women who are waiting to hear how God redeemed your story for his glory.

Take a deep breath, now let it out. And let the following words penetrate your soul.

ENCOUNTER GOD

My dearest one, I invite you to live boldly and bravely as you face your past and choose to step into your future. The fallen one attempted to destroy you. I promise to redeem every part of your history—the good, the bad, and the ugly. You will rise above the pain and encounter my love in new ways. I will redeem, restore, and rebuild you into my masterpiece. You are the cream of my crop. You are worthy. You are more than enough.

~Jesus
(John 10:10; Psalm 107:1–2, 43; Ephesians 2:10)

REACHING FOR MORE

Living bold and brave may seem impossible right now, yet you were brave when you gathered your courage and left him. The future is looming, yet you can step into it. You're getting stronger every day, yet your challenge is not to be strong in your own strength but in God's strength. You are becoming unstoppable.

1. What about the future scares you the most? Ask Jesus what he says about the future.
2. What is the difference between being a strong woman and a woman of strength? Which one are you right now?
3. When you think about surrender, what emotions and concerns do you have? After writing them out, ask Jesus what he wants to say about what you wrote.
4. Ask Jesus what he wants you to surrender. If you're ready, can you give it to him? When you release it, ask Jesus to fill you with the Holy Spirit and what he wants to give you in return (for example: hope, peace, joy, a new heart, a crown).
5. One day you will remember all your ex-husband did to you without the pain. That may be a long way off. For a moment I'd like you to write out what it may look like one day to be in a place where the memories don't haunt you.

CHAPTER 12

UNSTOPPABLE

Live Out the More

Some wandered in the wilderness, lost and homeless. Hungry and thirsty, they nearly died. "LORD, help!" they cried in their trouble, and he rescued them from their distress. He led them straight to safety, to a city where they could live.

—Psalm 107:4–7

There is hope for your future.

—Jeremiah 31:17

Healing is grueling. It can feel as if you're driving from New York to Los Angeles in one long stretch. You could be, at times, speeding down the freeway at eighty miles per hour, other times puttering behind great-grandpa, stuck in traffic, or lost because you missed your exit, all in the span of a few hours. You'll reach your destination but it's not a straight shot. You can drive coast to coast in two days if you take I-40 and don't stop, but that is impossible because you need to eat, fuel your vehicle, sleep, take bathroom breaks, and stretch your legs.

Healing, however, is more like driving the scenic route, taking your time, seeing the sights, stopping for the night, taking breaks, and getting lost.

Although I wrote this book's chapters in a certain order, healing doesn't follow formulas like 1, 2, 3 . . . My goal is to show you how principles of the Word and encounters with God that changed my life can change yours too. The truths in Scripture never change:

- He is your hope (Psalm 33:20).
- He is trustworthy (Psalm 18:30).
- He is close to the brokenhearted (Psalm 34:18).
- He will win you back when you've given up (Hosea 2:14).
- He will speak to you (John 10:1–5).
- He is your strong tower (Proverbs 18:10).
- He covers you with his wings (Psalm 17:8).
- He gathers your tears (Psalm 56:8).
- He will redeem your story (Psalm 107:43).
- He loves you more than he hates domestic abuse and divorce (Isaiah 54:10; Romans 8:38–39).
- He loves you more . . .

How do I know he loves you more? The Bible says so: "Mostly what God does is love you. Keep company with him and learn a life of love. Observe how Christ loved us. His love was not cautious but extravagant. He didn't love in order to get something from us but to give everything of himself to us. Love like that" (Ephesians 5:2 MSG).

Don't beat yourself up if you slow or stop your healing by avoiding the pain, burying it, or pretending it doesn't exist. There will be times when you are exhausted and need to rest. God wants you to rest just as he did after he created the world (Genesis 2:1–3). Rest is also included in the Ten Commandments and throughout Scripture.

One day you'll be exhausted from being a victim and being identified by others as one. You may believe it makes you weak and vulnerable. As I mentioned before, no one wants to be seen as weak. Although Scripture says, "For when I am weak, then I am strong" (2 Corinthians 12:10), *weak* refers to the state of being weakened—you've been weakened through the constant assault of abuse which made you a victim.

> The Bible consists of story after story of victims and how God redeemed their lives.

We've all been a victim at some point in our lives since we've all been hurt by someone. The Bible consists of story after story of victims and how God redeemed their lives. Each story has its own twist. God doesn't think less of the broken. He heals the broken and shattered so he can change the outcome of what was done to you.

ELEVEN DAYS TO NOWHERE

Normally it takes only eleven days to travel from Mount Sinai to Kadesh, going by way of Mount Seir. Yet Deuteronomy 1:3 tells us forty years after the Israelites left Egypt, they arrived in Canaan. So what should have taken eleven days to walk to the promised land took them *forty years.*

Why?

Numbers 13 tells the story of how the Israelites limited God and refused to enter the land. They didn't trust him, even though he'd proven himself trustworthy.

The Lord told Moses to pick a leader from each of the twelve tribes of Israel to spy out the land they were about to enter and bring back samples of the food being grown to give the people a taste for their new home. The spies explored the land for forty days and returned with luscious grapes, pomegranates, and figs and stories of bounty—it truly was a land flowing with milk and honey. But ten of the twelve leaders reported:

The people are powerful.

Their towns are fortified.

There are giants.

We are weak.

The giants are *giant.*

We are small.

We're grasshoppers in a land of giants.

Two spies, Joshua and Caleb, said yes, but "Let's go at once to take the land. . . . We can certainly conquer it!" (Numbers 13:30).

The ten spies apparently forgot all God did to rescue them from bondage and said, "We can't go up against them! They are stronger than we are!" Fear spread among the people as they listened to the lies that the land would devour them and the giants were giant. "Next to them we felt like grasshoppers, and that's what they thought, too!" (Numbers 13:31, 33).

Fear always makes the abuser look more powerful than God.

Numbers 14 recounts the rebellion of the people as they allowed fear to overshadow all the miracles they saw of the presence of God protecting and providing for them. They complained and accused Moses and God, and plotted to go back to their abusers. They wouldn't listen to Joshua and Caleb, who reminded them of what they saw and that God was with them and not to be afraid. The people believed the giants were more powerful than God, so they wanted to stone Joshua and Caleb. Fear always makes the abuser look more powerful than God.

Has fear of your husband outweighed your trust in God's ability to rescue you and redeem your life? Think back over your marriage. Can you see how your husband used fear to distort how you saw him, God, and yourself?

Guy made himself an idol in my life. He purposely replaced God, and I came to believe he was more powerful than God. I grumbled and complained against God, blamed him for not rescuing me, thought God was more concerned that Guy got right with Jesus, and believed I was unimportant except as a tool to be used to help my husband be a better man.

What kept Israel out of the promised land? Their complaints about being freed from bondage, believing they were better off as slaves. Murmuring against God, they were discontented and dissatisfied with him, even though he rescued them from bondage, killed their enemies, and gave them their own land filled with milk and honey. In simple terms, after all they saw him do on their behalf, they didn't believe his future promises of provision and protection.

Psalm 106:24 says, "The people refused to enter the pleasant land, for they wouldn't believe his promise to care for them."

The word *refused* means "to reject." It means limiting or avoiding association. In other words, the people limited and avoided associating with God by refusing to enter the land. They didn't believe God's promise to watch over and protect them. I understand their reaction. The Egyptians made themselves Israel's god by providing all the Israelites' basic necessities to keep them enslaved and alive so they could work. Though they were treated harshly, they were also cared for. Israel depended on their masters for everything.

I don't know about you, but I can identify with the Israelites. We know the end of the story—that God did, indeed, give them the promised land—but they didn't know the end. They saw terrifying giants firmly rooted in the land God gave them. It was much like me when I was first learning to live after I left Guy. While I was free from abuse physically, I wasn't always free of the lies whispered in my ear that I wasn't good enough, strong enough, and that God could never take my life and make it all work together for good.

We can hinder our healing by limiting God, and avoid him by blaming him for the abuse, for allowing us to get married, and for not making our spouses godly men. You may even think after the marriage is over that God is blessing your ex-husband because he has moved on to another woman, created a new family, lives in a new or bigger house, and so on, while you struggle to survive.

BeLoved, this is all a lie from the fallen one. He twists what you see and how you see. There comes a time, even when it seems God isn't trustworthy, when we must turn to God. James 4:8 says, "Draw near to God and He will draw near to you" (NASB). What a beautiful promise from the heart of the Father.

Israel wandered in the wilderness for forty years until every man and woman twenty years old and older who came out of Egypt died, except for Joshua and Caleb. The Israelite children were raised with a slave mindset. The children had to learn how not to live as slaves, but as free people. So again, what should have taken eleven days took forty years.

They could not possess the land and all that would entail by thinking like slaves. They had to own the promise of their future as free people.

In this story, you can either focus on the ten who twisted what they saw and limited God, or you can follow the lead of Joshua and Caleb, who agreed there were giants in the land but believed they could take them because God was on their side.

You might be like me and go back and forth between the two ways to focus. Some days you might feel God is strong enough to slay your giants. But other days, when it appears life is harder for you than your ex-husband, you may feel you're being punished and he's being blessed.

The Psalms are full of back-and-forth rants against God and evil. In some of David's songs, you'll find him asking God why he's been deserted, then praising the only one who could rescue him. In other songs, the writer asks if God is listening to his cries of pain, then wonders when the evil will suffer as he has, especially those who claim to love God. In all these psalms, though, the songwriter comes back to praise, acknowledging that God is the only one who can help him.

What's the takeaway here? You can turn against the only one who can help you, or like a child with a skinned knee, you can run into his arms for comfort.

THE LAND OF MORE

After the Israelites wandered for forty years, God led them to the Jordan River. Once they crossed over, they would be in the promised land, what I call the "land of more." Joshua 1 details God's instructions and promises. First, he charged Joshua to lead the people after Moses died and to remember that the promises he made to Moses, he will keep with Joshua. The promises have two parts: God's part and the people's part. God will only do his part; the people can't do God's part, and he won't do their part.

Here's a visual of what that looked like in Joshua's story so you can relate to it in your situation, as well.

God's Part	Our Part
Wherever you go, you'll be on land I gave you.	Be strong and courageous.
No one can stand against you.	Be strong and very courageous.
I will be with you.	Obey God's instruction.

God's Part	Our Part
I will not fail you.	Do not deviate from it.
I will not abandon you.	Study the Word.
I will be with you wherever you go.	Meditate on the Word.
You will be successful in all you do.	Obey what is written.
You will prosper and succeed in all you do.	Be strong and courageous.
The Lord is with you wherever you go.	Do not be afraid or discouraged.

Are you sensing a theme and redundancy? How many times does God need to tell us to be strong and courageous? Maybe until we get what he's saying? Notice there are also some things he left out, such as:

- Don't do anything.
- You won't face trouble or enemies.
- You don't have to fight or battle.
- Life will be easy and pain free.
- You won't be afraid or discouraged.

After Joshua's conversation with the Lord—Can you imagine having an out-loud chat with God?—Joshua rallied the people to prepare to move into their future, and to remember all that Moses shared with them before he died. The people said they would do what they were told. Jumping ahead to Joshua 3:5, Joshua told them to purify themselves and get ready to cross over the Jordan the next day.

The Lord promised to make Joshua a great leader. He'd been Moses's number-two man for forty years. Moses was the rescuer, who delivered them from their past; Joshua was the warrior who would lead the Israelites into their future. For four decades, God protected the nation from danger, provided food when they were hungry, provided water when they were thirsty, and guided them through the land. Life for Israel was about to change. They would become participants in their freedom by learning to fight for victory.

The priests carried the ark of the covenant, stepped a few feet into the raging Jordan River, and stopped. As they wiggled their toes in the rushing river, the flow of the water slowed until the riverbed was dry. This was different than crossing the Red Sea when the water parted in front of them. The Jordan River walled up a great distance away in a town called Adam. The water flowing downstream rushed into the Dead Sea until they could walk across (Joshua 3:16).

The priests then stood in the middle of the river with the ark of the covenant as the people crossed over into their future—a scary unknown future with giants.

"Today you will know that the living God is among you" (Joshua 3:10). What a powerful promise that isn't just for Israel; it is for all of us today who trust in him. It's what I love about Scripture. It's not just a history book, but a living book that applies to us today. Just as Israel had to battle after they entered the promised land, so do we.

We have an enemy whom I refer to as the fallen one. He also knows God's promises; he's read the book. He's made a few declarations too:

- Did God really say . . . ? (Genesis 3:1)
- I will fight you and turn those closest to you against you.
- You will fail.
- You are a failure.
- You're unworthy.
- You're a slave.
- Who do you think you are?

And you wonder why we're repeatedly told in Scripture not to be afraid and to be courageous? Our battle really isn't against people. Our battle is with the fallen one. Ephesians 6:12 reads: "For we are not fighting against flesh-and-blood enemies, but against evil rulers and authorities of the unseen world, against mighty powers in this dark world, and against evil spirits in the heavenly places."

The majority of the book of Joshua is about Israel conquering the land that was already theirs. Prior to each battle Israel faced, Joshua asked God what they should do. He was basically asking for a battle plan. When he asked for and executed God's plan, they experienced victory. When he didn't, they failed or were duped.

There are no promises life will be easy, but if we seek the Lord, we will conquer the land and the hurdles the fallen one puts in our way. Sometimes success is living to fight another day.

The land of more is the place where the impossible happens, where the sun stands still, where battles are won, where every place you step becomes yours. That doesn't mean it's easy—it's not—but we are worth fighting for.

TIME TO BATTLE

BeLoved, you aren't alone in this battle to take back your life and step into your future. God is close to you even though he may feel far away. There are times you may need to lean back just a bit to feel his presence. Nothing is more comforting to me than when my husband, Tom, stands behind me. I'll lean back on him, feeling his heart beating as he wraps me in his arms. This is a picture of the presence of God.

Psalm 107 was my go-to Psalm when I first left my marriage. I reread the entire Psalm in preparation for writing this chapter and was amazed as I realized how well David described the loneliness of abuse. The psalm gives words to pain and hopelessness. It begins and ends with hope, much like us.

You began your marriage with hope until your fairy tale turned into a nightmare. Now God is saying he'll bring hope from your story, change the ending by writing a new future for you. There will be battles for your liberty as you break free from lies, pain, and shame.

Remember, Paul told us in Philippians 3:13 to "focus on this one thing: Forgetting the past and looking forward to what lies ahead." That doesn't mean the past isn't important and didn't impact us.

Our past isn't just about what happened to us, but about what God *does* with what happened to us.

But if all we do is focus on the past, we can get lost without directions to guide us forward. I'll repeat this until it sinks in: Our past isn't just about what happened to us, but about what God *does* with what happened to us.

Quite a few memories surfaced as I finished writing this book. If I dwell in those memories, they could pull me back into the pain of the past. Instead, I consider them reminders of what God brought me out of and the healing he's done in my life.

I remember the hopelessness I felt at the time, when the future looked like a black hole of pain. Hope sheds light on the future. I couldn't have imagined what my future looks like today. God gave me glimpses, but it wasn't enough to see the full picture.

BeLoved, you are unstoppable, and as you do your part, you can trust God to do his part. There is no courage without fear, so with trembling hands and shaky knees, stand strong and courageous because he is the one who knows what is ahead. He will give you strength, mercy, and grace when you need it.

"Now all glory to God, who is able, through his mighty power at work within us, to accomplish infinitely more than we might ask or think" (Ephesians 3:20). Are you ready for the "infinitely more" God has for you? Then rejoice, because the season of darkness is turning to a season of light.

This promise in Song of Songs 2:11 is for you, my friend: "The season has changed, the bondage of your barren winter has ended, and the season of hiding is over and gone. The rains have soaked the earth" (TPT). Rains bring new growth and new life. Live yours unstoppably.

ENCOUNTER GOD

My darling daughter, your season is changing, shifting before your eyes. Trust me to bring beauty out of the ugly. Choose to live a life without limitations as you step into your promised land.

Don't allow complaints and blame to keep you chained to your past. I promise to be your strength, your hope, and your future. I will defend and protect you as you battle for freedom. Trust me to accomplish all I said I would do for you and in you. Trust me to bring purpose out of your story. Be strong and courageous, meditate on my Word, and trust my love for you.

~Jesus
(Isaiah 61:3; Ephesians 3:20;
Philippians 2:14; 1:6; Joshua 1:7–9)

REACHING FOR MORE

Living as unstoppable and without limitations may look like a long shot after the one who should have loved you stopped you at every turn, bending you to his will. Now you're learning how to seek God's will for you and learning to receive from him.

1. Write out what it would look like to receive love and goodness from God.
2. How has your view of yourself and God changed? How do you want it to change?
3. What are the giants you want to overcome?
4. The land of more is an enchanting place where the impossible can happen. List out what looks impossible in your land called More. Ask God for a promise to go with the impossible.
5. Write out your hopes and dreams for your future; make them outrageous and audacious.

ANOTHER ONE FREE

At last we have freedom, for Christ has set us free! We must always cherish this truth and firmly refuse to go back into the bondage of our past.

—Galatians 5:1 (TPT)

Let me tell you about my Jesus.

I first heard about Jesus a month after I turned fifteen. I wasn't impressed and didn't really like him much. His Dad was mean and exacting, Jesus was the killer of fun and . . . Holy Spirit *who*? I wasn't excited to attend church since my first experience five years earlier didn't turn out well for me. It's where a church member molested me.

I became a poser, pretending to be into the church life to keep my mom happy. I watched fellow churchgoers to learn how to sound and look Christian. What I didn't know was that this Jesus was in pursuit of a leery, weary girl. He heard my mother's plea for her wayward daughter whom she knew was in trouble, but didn't know why.

Just two months shy of my seventeenth birthday, Jesus introduced himself to me at a Dave Wilkerson rally in Anaheim, California. I liked what I heard about him and was slightly surprised that he seemed different from the Jesus I heard about at my church. At the end of the meeting, the audience was invited to come to the front if we wanted to meet Jesus. I felt compelled to meet this extraordinary Jesus. That night he became a part of my life and changed me forever.

If you're not sure you know Jesus, I'd love to introduce you to him. He loves you just as you are. You can talk to him now if you like. If you're not sure what to say to him, you can say this prayer with me:

Jesus, your Word says, "For all have sinned and fall short of the glory of God" (Romans 3:23 ESV), and I ask you to forgive me. I believe you died for my sins and took my penalty upon yourself and then rose from the grave. I invite you to come into my heart, to transform my life, and to heal my broken heart. I choose to follow you as my Lord and Savior. Thank you, Jesus, for coming into my life. Amen.

But wait! There's more

When I got saved, I thought, *This is it, I'm going to heaven!* Thirty-seven years later when I began attending a large church in Texas, I learned there was more to salvation, more to asking Jesus into my life, more than going to heaven.

The Bible says, "Whoever will call on the name of the Lord will be saved" (Romans 10:13 NASB).

The word *saved* in the Greek is *sozo*. It means more than being saved and going to heaven; it's not just salvation from your sins, but being saved or delivered from harm or illness, deliverance from death and sin, physical and emotional healing. To *be saved* means living, healed, set free, and delivered. You and I are *saved* for all time once we ask Jesus into our life. We are *being saved* on a daily basis through healing, set free from the chains of our past, and delivered from anything that would keep us in bondage.

Throughout my Christian walk, I was taught that life was something to be endured until you get to heaven. I was fifty-four, and my world was about to change. If I'd known what was coming, I might have been just a little afraid. Instead, I started on a journey to discover every aspect of salvation.

BeLoved, you don't have to live the remainder of your life with the damage from domestic violence. It's not a life sentence. Healing is something you choose to pursue like searching for wisdom, gold, or lost car keys.

Jesus came to set us free from sin and death. He also came to deliver us from evil and to heal us. Jesus healed thousands and thousands, among them the blind, deaf, those with broken bodies, those with bleeding bodies. He raised the dead, among them men, women, children, young and old, rich and poor, religious and not. Demons bowed in his presence, darkness was dispelled. He turned water into wine, he gave life to those who were dead—emotionally and physically. He transformed most of those he interacted with.

He's gentle, kind, compassionate, firm, direct, and meek. Don't mistake meek for weak or mousy; meekness is power under authority. Jesus humbled himself and came to this earth as a baby, fully God, fully man. While he walked this earth, he deferred to his Father; he didn't access his authority as God. He came to be one of us.

STAY FREE

Jesus set us free, but *staying* free is up to us. We choose every day either to live in freedom or to fall back into the bondage from which he set us free. Some days you may find yourself bouncing between the two. You aren't perfect, so give yourself grace and mercy.

Freedom is free, but it's not easy.

Have you ever watched a video of a child learning to walk? They stand, lose balance, squat, straighten up, take an unsteady step, fall on their behind, sit for a second while slightly confused, get up, and start all over again. They are determined to move, to master this walking thing. Somehow, the baby understands there is freedom in walking, and once he or she walks, they can outrun Mommy.

Freedom is free, but it's not easy.

Daniel 3 tells the story of Hananiah, Mishael, and Azariah. You may know them by their Babylonians names: Shadrach, Meshach, and Abednego. I will refer to them as the Hebrew Three.

In the story, Nebuchadnezzar made a gold statue of himself so the people could worship him. Sounds a bit narcissistic, right? When he heard that the Hebrew Three refused to worship his idol, Scripture says he "flew into a rage" (Daniel 3:13). Nebuchadnezzar told the Hebrew Three, "And then what god will be able to rescue you from *my* power?" (verse 15, emphasis added). Isn't that how an abuser thinks? He makes himself all-powerful and expects you to worship him because he has all the power.

I love the response of the Hebrew Three, "O Nebuchadnezzar, we do not need to defend ourselves before you. *If* we are thrown into the blazing furnace, the God whom we serve is *able* to save us. *He will* rescue us from your power, Your Majesty. But *even if* he doesn't, we want to make it clear to you, Your Majesty, that *we will never* serve your gods or worship the gold statue you have set up" (verses 16–18, emphasis added). Nebuchadnezzar again became so furious that his face was distorted with rage.

This scenario sounds so familiar. The sadness is that I gave up my power bit by bit as Guy conditioned me to think he was all-powerful. I had more fear of my abuser than I had faith in God's power to rescue me. Fear steals our power and sound mind. Now we are taking back our power through Jesus, who is love.

We are taking back our power through Jesus, who is love.

Here is the rest of the story of the Hebrew Three: "'Look!' Nebuchadnezzar shouted. 'I see four men, unbound, walking around in the fire unharmed! And the fourth looks like a god!'" (verse 25). This is a powerful picture of the healing journey. Even when you are in the fire of pain, anxiety, and turmoil from your abuser, Jesus is always with you. The Hebrew Three came out of the fire unbound, unsinged, unscorched, and unsmoked! As if they'd never been in the fire. Bam!

You can live as Another One Free.

DON'T STOP, THERE'S MORE...

HOW DOES GOD KNOW WHAT IT FEELS LIKE TO BE A WOMAN?

The woman who asked me this question had endured a horrific childhood that followed her into adulthood and manifested in addiction, domestic violence, and more. Her question stopped me. Normally I have an answer (most times I *think* I have the answer), but this question stumped me. It wasn't something I'd thought about or questioned until then. I didn't know the answer; only God could answer this question. Emergency prayer resulted in this response:

"God created man in His own image, in the image of God He created him; male and female He created them" (Genesis 1:27 NASB).

"Then the LORD God formed man of dust from the ground, and breathed into his nostrils the breath of life; and man became a living being" (Genesis 2:7 NASB).

I have a fairly active imagination. I picture God scooping up a handful of dirt and spitting into his hand as he began molding dirt like clay into a human being, pulling, twisting, smoothing, using his fingernail to create detail. I imagine he had a hint of a smile as he admired his creation and was delighted to see his creation take a breath as he breathed his breath and himself into a person.

Abba God.

God is one, yet three, the triune God. I'm not going to attempt to explain this unexplainable mystery, though many have written whole books about the Trinity. The three are the Father, Son (Jesus), and Holy Spirit. YHWH, Elohim, El Shaddai, and Adonai are a few names used for God. I think his favorite name is Abba God, translated as Daddy God. It's Jesus's favorite name for his Father. When I use the term God, I'm referring to all three.

God put into Adam both masculine and feminine traits since Adam was created in the image of God. Scriptures are filled with the "mother" characteristics and analogies of God. Here are a few verses that reveal the motherly side of God:

- God clearly identified with a mother's love when he said, "Can a mother forget her nursing child? Can she feel no love for the child she has borne? But even if that were possible, I would not forget you!" (Isaiah 49:15).
- David, who knew God intimately, likened his relationship with God to that of a child with its mother when he said: "I have calmed and quieted myself, like a weaned child who no longer cries for its mother's milk. Yes, like a weaned child is my soul within me" (Psalm 131:2).
- Jesus compared his love for his people to that of a mother hen desperate for her chicks: "How often I have wanted to gather your children together as a hen protects her chicks beneath her wings, but you wouldn't let me" (Matthew 23:37).

God understands what it is to be a woman. "The LORD God fashioned into a woman the rib which He had taken from the man, and brought her to the man" (Genesis 2:22 NASB). God fashioned and designed the woman, He took his time with her so she'd be a perfect fit for Adam. Does God know what it's like to be a woman? Absolutely. He could only put into her what is in him. Though some in the church may treat women as lesser than men, Genesis 2:22 is a reminder that God doesn't see women that way.

All this happened after Adam was given the task of naming the animals. By the time he finished, Adam recognized there was no one like him; all the creatures had a partner except him. How like God to use the unusual to reveal to Adam that he was alone, which God saw as "not good" (Genesis 2:18).

God knew Adam needed someone similar to him. Woman wasn't created as less than Adam but to be his *ezer neged*. I'll say it this way, based on the Hebrew meaning of *ezer neged*—the woman is Adam's help and strength. She has his back and corresponds to and is his equal. *Ezer* is also used for God as our helper: Exodus 18:4; Deuteronomy 33:7, 26, 29; Psalms 20:2; 33:20; 70:5; 115:9–11; 121:1–2; 124:8; 146:5; and Hosea 13:9. God created her to become Eve, the mother of all.

Does God know what it's like to be a woman? Oh yes.

JESUS

Jesus came to earth as a boy child. So how could Jesus know what it's like to be a woman? He never experienced cramps or PMS, being ogled or used for his body. He wasn't seen as "lesser than" as the women were in his day. Though born a boy, he is fully God and fully man, so in an odd sense he knew. I will not attempt to explain; it's beyond my knowledge. I've realized over the years that no one can explain everything about God. He is far beyond explanation.

According to John 1:3, "God created everything through him, and nothing was created except through him." Jesus was there when Adam and Eve were created. As you read through the Gospels, you'll see the compassion and tenderness of Jesus toward women. He gave women a voice, called them out, healed them, forgave them.

John 20:15–18 records Jesus's interaction with Mary Magdalene after his resurrection. The moment he called her by her name melts my heart every time I read it. Jesus went out of his way to connect with women, he treated each woman with honor and respect, even the women with less than stellar reputations.

Does Jesus know what it's like to be a woman? Yes, he does, even though I don't completely understand how. You might think I'm arrogant if I told you I asked him this unusual question. Instead of words, he showed me a visual of himself smiling and laughing.

HOLY SPIRIT

The Holy Spirit is nurturing and motherly, ever the comforter; peace, grace, and mercy flow from the Holy Spirit. Does the Holy Spirit know what it's like to be a woman? Without a doubt.

If you wonder about God's ability to understand what it is to be a woman, remember that he's the one who created you and put femininity into you.

Invite Jesus into your secret place—have a conversation with him about you as a woman. I think you'll be surprised and delighted by what he says.

YOUR PICKER ISN'T BROKEN

Are you beginning to think your picker is broken? Does it seem as if you date the same guy but with different skin over and over? Or you may not be interested in finding another man after what you survived. It may be too soon. Don't let anyone rush you into a relationship you're not ready for.

These are some of the comments I've heard from women:

"I married the same type of man three times."

"I seem to be attracted to the bad boys."

"I just can't pick them. I always pick the unattainable man."

But what if your picker isn't broken? What if your picker just needs to be healed so you can recognize the predators? Predators see beauty in brokenness. To them, it says you survived abuse, how much more would you put up with? Because of the trauma you survived, you have a strength many women don't have.

If you're a church girl, your foundational beliefs about forgiveness, second chances, standing by your man, not complaining about your spouse, marriage being for life, turning the other cheek, and submission, to name a few, make you attractive to a predator. None of those beliefs or values are bad. In a healthy marriage, they are good. But in an abusive or narcissistic marriage they are weapons used to keep you trapped in a never-ending cycle of hell.

This is the part missing from dating handbooks and premarital counseling. Our church leaders and pastors aren't taught in seminary how to handle abuse or what it looks like. They tend to believe abuse is a *marriage* problem when it's a *heart* problem.

Abusers are chameleons; they blend in with their surroundings. They can adapt their behavior and speech to fit in at church or at a bar. Most people would describe them as charming, charismatic, likeable, and confident—which is the image they project. In reality they are self-absorbed, arrogant, entitled, and lack empathy. This is the side they generally won't reveal until after marriage.

In the dating phase, they will focus on you, make you feel special and valued, and they'll invite you to share your deepest darkest secrets, feigning empathy. They'll probe to discover boundaries and nonnegotiables, not so they can honor them but so they know where to apply pressure. You believe your boundaries and nonnegotiables are your strength, but predators see them as your weakness and a challenge to get you to break your own beliefs and boundaries.

There are signs of abuse in the dating process but if you don't know to look for the red flags you will miss them. And what is the difference between a red flag and a flawed human? Let's face it, none of us is perfect; we all have flaws and shortcomings. We all come into a relationship with some baggage. If you're looking for the perfect man, you'll be disappointed.

Knowing the difference between red flags, which warn of danger, and shortcomings, or areas that need healing, is important before you get too far into a relationship. That is where wisdom comes in and the need to pay attention to how you are treated.

Proverbs 2:1–4 holds the key to wisdom, without which we can be fooled by a person pretending to be someone they are not. The keys to wisdom are:

- Treasure God's Word: read and study the Word.
- Tune your ear to wisdom: listen to his voice because what God says never violates his written Word or his character.
- Cry out and ask: ask the Lord for understanding and insight so you can see and hear clearly.
- Search for understanding and insight: if you lost a diamond ring, you would tear apart your house to find it, you'd ask others to pray for you to find it. Do the same to get the insight you need.

Verses 5–8 hold the promise of wisdom for those who seek for it. God promises to guard and protect you when you seek wisdom. Oh how I wish I knew this truth as a young believer. It would have saved me from so much heartache.

Proverbs 2:12–15 gives us an outline on how to see beyond what someone is presenting:

> Wisdom will save you from evil people,
>   from those whose words are twisted.
> These men turn from the right way
>   to walk down dark paths.
> They take pleasure in doing wrong,
>   and they enjoy the twisted ways of evil.
> Their actions are crooked,
>   and their ways are wrong.

That is the best dating advice. Without wisdom we will only see what a person presents, not what is hidden. Predators use tactics like love bombing to keep you distracted when they push your boundaries. For example, you may say you don't want to kiss right away, and he will agree and seem to honor your choice. But then one night, he asks for a kiss. You'll say no, not yet. Slowly he will become relentless, wearing you down, and you won't realize it because it looks and sounds like love and desire. And who doesn't want to be wanted and desired?

Once he breaks you down with something as small as a kiss, he'll move on to your next boundary all the while speaking words of affirmation and kindness to you. When you give in, you'll believe it was your idea. He may even stop you and say, "No, let's wait," and next time it will be you asking for the kiss. That's when he looks like the hero because he said *wait* and you said *go*. Can you see the manipulation?

An abuser will affirm you by telling you how special you are, then let you know, subtly, how you're not enough, then reaffirm that he's never met anyone like you. Unless you're paying attention, you won't hear the covert put down and how he really feels about you.

It is important to pay attention to how you feel when you're with him and how you feel when you're not. If you pay attention, you'll sense the Holy Spirit warning you, though it may feel like an uneasiness in the pit of your stomach.

Keep your secrets, deepest hurts, trauma, and dreams to yourself. In other words, be careful about being vulnerable too soon while dating, until you know he's trustworthy to keep your heart safe. Remember, an abuser wants to learn your deepest wounds and your deepest longings so he can use that knowledge to get what he wants from you. He may even share something intimate from his past to get you to open up.

The Scriptures tell us to guard our hearts. That's great wisdom, especially until you know his intentions. Matthew 7:6 instructs, "Don't waste what is holy on people who are unholy. Don't throw your pearls to pigs! They will trample the pearls, then turn and attack you."

MAN-HATER

Man-hater was branded across my forehead for about five years. Anytime a man even looked in my direction, I gave him what I call my ugly face (although I didn't realized that's what I was doing at the time). It was a warning to not come close, like a porcupine ready to hurl deadly quills. That face served me well for five years, until God brought Tom Gardner into my life. I discovered a new kind of terror—dating in your fifties. It's not like riding a bike and it's not the same as when you were in high school or in your twenties.

My first husband was in law enforcement. Most police officers tend to look down on those in private security, seeing them as wannabe cops. I admit I had the same attitude when Tom told me what he did for a living. I soon discovered that Tom isn't a wannabe anything. He's a bodyguard. Bodyguards watch for danger in order to get their client away before danger gets close. Law enforcement officers react to danger after it happens; they aren't usually called until there is a problem. Tom carries himself with confidence, is well-spoken, and kind. I was leery. He seemed too good to be true.

I wasn't sure I wanted to get married again, especially when I called it the M-word. One day God said he wanted to give me a husband. *What? Why?* His response: *It's the one area in which you don't trust me.* There were actually more areas in which I didn't trust, but he was planting an idea in me that I was far from being ready for. A month later, while on a getaway, I asked God about this husband. *I'm getting him ready for you*, he seemed to be saying. Cryptic.

I wasn't sure I could ever trust another man again. God wasn't just preparing Tom, He was preparing *me*.

It would be another two years before I met Tom. In the meantime, God began teaching me to see God himself as my husband (Isaiah 54:5). If this feels weird or offensive to you, then move on. It's okay that you're not ready to see God this way.

At one point, I tried to make a list of what I wanted in a husband, and I felt God ask, *What are you doing?* I tore it up. Through the years I'd heard plenty of sermons about what a woman of God looks like, but I don't remember hearing any about what a man of God looks like.

A few months prior to meeting Tom, I asked the Lord what a man of God looked like, and he took me to 1 Samuel 16:14–18. The gist of the story is that Saul no longer had the Spirit of God, he now had a tormenting spirit which would send him into a rage. His servants suggested they find someone to play music to soothe him. When Saul agreed, they said, we know a guy. The guy was a young David who had just been anointed as king to replace Saul. Young David was described this way: he plays well, he's a man of valor, a warrior, he speaks well, he's good-looking, and the Lord is with him. There you have it, sweet and simple. It seemed like a far-fetched goal for any man, much like the description of the "ideal wife" in Proverbs 31 is for women.

As I got to know Tom, those six ideals or characteristics would run through my mind, and over time I saw him live out each one. I still couldn't say the word *marriage* or see myself married, not because there was anything wrong with Tom, but because I didn't think I could do it again. I'd say, "I can see spending my life with you." That's a close as I got to the subject of marriage.

HE PLAYS WELL

1 Samuel 16:17 refers to music, and I'm not saying a godly man should be musical. The verse explains that he "plays well." My first thought when I read it was he had a good sense of humor and gets along

with others. Who doesn't want a man who knows how to have fun? I watched Tom as he interacted with my family and friends and how they responded to him. He interacted with other women differently than how he treated me. But Tom didn't reveal his full sense of humor until after we married. It was a delightful surprise.

HE'S A MAN OF VALOR

A man of God is also a man of honor and integrity in all he does—at his job, when he tips, and even the way he serves.

A godly man will treat you with honor and integrity when no one is around and in front of others. He won't push your boundaries, he'll honor them. He won't probe you to learn your past hurts, mistakes, or deepest longings. When you are ready to share, he'll keep your secrets and not use them as weapons against you.

He is brave and courageous and stands up for what he believes in, not shy about being a Jesus follower. He's a gentleman. Tom still opens doors for me, including the car door, and pulls out my chair at restaurants. When we met he was an all-around gentleman . . . and he still is.

HE'S A WARRIOR

A man of God is courageous, he's willing to fight for you and himself, he doesn't run when life gets difficult. He protects your relationship, guards your physical relationship. He would not only die for you, he will live for you by becoming the man God calls him to be and continuing his own healing journey.

Tom and I had a long conversation about our physical relationship and what it should look like. Neither one of us wanted sex outside of marriage; we wanted to honor God in our relationship. After our conversation on how to keep pure, I asked God about it and I felt his response was, *Leave it to Tom*. The next day I told Tom and he said, "Oh no. You set the boundaries, and I'll honor them." I didn't know what to do with that, this was uncharted territory. I will tell you he never once pushed my boundaries, and I was careful to honor him too.

A godly man is also a champion; he's willing to be the man God called him to be. It's not that he should change for you, but he'll pursue healing. He won't blame you for his mistakes or devalue you. He'll be your biggest support.

HE SPEAKS WELL

He's well-spoken, he doesn't mock or belittle you, he speaks life into you. He doesn't use foul or abusive language. His words will build you up, not flatter you. His words affirm you, and he won't tear you down to build himself up. His words honor you and others, including servers at dinner.

Tom seemed almost too good to be true. I watched and listened to him to see if he was really the man he projected. He's not perfect—he'll apologize when he's wrong. The night he told me he loved me, I was stunned to silence. I asked him if he was okay that I couldn't tell him how I felt, especially since I didn't know how I felt. He was okay with it and said he wasn't expecting a response. He knew I was as skittish as a newborn colt and was afraid I might run.

A couple days later I asked him, "*Why* do you love me?" His response floored me, as he told me what he valued about me, the qualities he saw in me, my relationship with God. He loved me for who I was, not for what I looked like. His words said he didn't want to *get* something from me but to *give* love to me.

HE'S GOOD-LOOKING

This one is relative. A godly man may not be drop-dead gorgeous; however, if he has these godly characteristics and qualities, he will be attractive no matter what he looks like. Also, a man of God is not consumed with his looks, but does take care of himself and loves himself in a healthy way. If a man doesn't love himself, he can't love others, including you.

THE LORD IS WITH HIM

This is the most important attribute. A man can have the first five qualities, but if the Lord isn't with him, nothing else matters. The Bible uses the phrase "and the Lord was with him" about Isaac, Joshua, Gideon, David, Solomon, and even Mary the mother of Jesus, to name a few.

People can talk about God, quote Scripture, pray, do ministry, go to church, and not know Jesus. Ezekiel 33:31 says, "So my people come pretending to be sincere and sit before you. They listen to your words, but they have no intention of doing what you say. Their mouths are full of lustful words, and their hearts seek only after money [gain made through violence]."

Is Jesus in his heart? Does his walk match his talk?

DON'T DATE IN SECRET

Tom and I agreed to be accountable to other people while we dated. Tom would talk with my brother, Ron, about our relationship. Ron asked Tom if he was willing to take on my baggage—I had a lot of baggage from my previous marriage. Tom was willing. Ron asked me if I was ready to get married. Let's just say I ran my answer around the bush a few times without answering. Mind you this was early in our relationship.

I talked with Monica, a close friend, and Deb, my sister-in-law, several times a week. They both had permission to be open and honest with me. Tom came to all my family gatherings and sat with the family at church. It didn't take long for them to fall in love with him. I think they fell in love with him before I did.

When I speak with women who are tired of dating or marrying the same kind of guy over and over, they often tell me that friends or family would warn them against the guy, but they didn't listen and they weren't sure why they didn't listen to them. There are a couple reasons for that: they may not have given anyone permission to speak truth to them, or friends may have approached them in a way they couldn't hear. Generally, their advice would be the opposite of what others would tell them, that he was a good guy. They would also say they aren't sure why they didn't listen when friends and family tried to warn them.

Why two different views of the same guy? It was often someone in ministry who said the abuser was a good guy, because that is the persona he presented. Also, keep in mind that if you share with an abuser what your friend said negatively about him, he may love bomb you to distract you, reminding you that you're the woman of his dreams. He will eventually isolate you from the people who spoke against him.

One question I should have asked God before I married Guy was, "Is this the man you want for me?" It never occurred to me to ask God questions about Guy.

TALK OR MAKE OUT

Tom and I were overly careful with our physical relationship. We didn't go to each other's apartments, not because we didn't trust each other but because we didn't want there to be any question about the integrity of our relationship. What we did is talk, a lot, all the time, at a coffee shop, in a park, walking, after a movie, or in a sitting area at a fancy hotel.

We saw others make the mistake of getting physical too soon and then they stopped talking and stopped learning about each other. The relationship becomes more about how you make each other feel which also makes it difficult to see any glaring red flags. Plus, it can cause you to stop seeking wisdom and hearing from God.

Tom and I have been married more than ten years, and we still talk. We enjoy each other's company. We share things with each other, knowing we won't use that information as a weapon against one another. We have had moments when we've reminded each other of our flaws. But we learned to forgive quickly and not hold on to the offense, which is hard. My brother says often, "Do you want to be right or have relationship?" Some of us want both.

If I make it sound like our marriage is perfect, it isn't. We have our moments of frustration, miscommunication, and irritation. We embrace loving through the hard. Some of our roughest times were when one of us was triggered. Our marriage brought us both to a deeper level of healing as we worked through the triggers. When you think you're healed, you'll discover a whole new level of healing in marriage.

LONELINESS VERSUS ALONENESS

When you're single, loneliness can feel like isolation, desolation, and emptiness. Loneliness is a pit we can fall into that at first feels warm and fuzzy, but can lead us to the land of desolation and desperation. It's a place where we don't make good decisions, and it can blind us from what we need to see. Loneliness can be overwhelming after you leave your abuser. In a sense you may be addicted to the chaos and trauma, not because of you but because this was your life. Give yourself grace and mercy to adjust to new beginnings.

Aloneness can feel like being comfortable in your skin and comfortable being alone. You enjoy solitude. You're not desperate to find a man. You can do what you want, when you want, without having to consider someone else. I've been in both these places while I was single. Loneliness was horrible and aloneness felt good, to the point that I questioned whether I wanted to stay single or marry again. Two months later, Tom walked into my life, and the rest is history.

I'm not saying you should get remarried if you haven't. If you think about remarriage and it sends shivers up your spine, you're not ready. It's okay. God will be all you need—protector and provider, lover and friend, confidant and companion.

Seek wisdom. Predators are like roaring lions seeking whom they can devour (1 Peter 5:8). Don't be fooled by those who make excuses for abusive behavior (Ephesians 5:6).

All in all, you got this, girl!

EIGHT QUESTIONS YOU DON'T HAVE TO ANSWER

But Jesus made no further answer.

—Mark 15:5 (ESV)

Have you ever felt you *needed* to respond when someone asked you a personal question? I always felt compelled to answer questions, even when I felt awkward or uncomfortable. A friend told me that just because someone asked a question didn't mean I had to answer it. Really? I was stunned, but I shouldn't have been.

There isn't an order to the questions below, and there may be more you could add. Each one of these questions implies that you could have changed the outcome and were in some way at fault for what your abuser did to you.

God created us to be inquisitive and to ask questions. But some questions should be neither asked nor answered. The questions below are insensitive, and the askers are clueless as to how it will impact you when they ask. Interviewers may ask one or all the questions, thinking they will help someone understand and answer all their whys. Instead, the questions slime you with shame. People aren't intentionally trying to shame you. They just don't know what they don't know.

1. Why did you stay?

   This question implies the asker would not have put up with the abuse for five minutes, would not have put themselves in your position, or they would have done better. The question leaves you feeling stupid for not leaving sooner.

   You can turn the question around and educate the asker with your answer. Some of the reasons women stay are finances, no place to go, fear of his response, or that no one will believe he's capable of being an abuser.

2. Why didn't you call the police?

   In my case, he *was* the police. Most of the time there aren't any bruises on your body since he used intimidation and the violence of his words to batter you. So it becomes a matter of "he said, she said" and the man is usually believed since he is calm and you're hysterical and unbalanced after the trauma. And you know that when he gets out of jail, he's coming for you, not the police.

3. Why didn't you tell someone?

   Who do you tell? Most women fear not being believed, and this is a real fear. Most people don't believe evil comes to church and quotes the Bible.

   And how do you tell someone the horrors you've been living through? You may have gone to your pastor only to be told to forgive and be a better and more submissive wife. Or you may have been accused of complaining about your husband or told to leave but you were terrified to leave. Where would you go?

4. Why didn't you see the red flags?

   He works his charming magic so you don't see the red flags. And we want to believe the best in people, so we become blinded to the warning signs.

5. Why did you marry him?

   You may wish you knew this answer. But it may take years for you to uncover the why.

6. Did you provoke him?

   Absolutely not! Crazy as it sounds, you may be asked this question.

7. Since you married him, wasn't there something good about him?

   How do you explain how he seemed kind and loving until you said "I do"? That the fairy tale turned into a nightmare.

8. Is it bad enough for a divorce?

   Yes. Or you wouldn't be here.

What is the moral of this story? You're not obligated to answer any of these or other questions you're not comfortable with. If you choose to respond, you might want to use any of the following:

- Why do you ask?
- I'm not ready to talk about it.
- I'm still processing.
- A better question to ask is how you can help.
- That's a question only he can answer. (Then just smile.)

GOD, CHURCH, AND ABUSE

I did talk about this subject in the book proper, but I also wanted to discuss it as a separate topic.

Some Christians are of the opinion that the Bible doesn't talk about abuse. I was one of them until I was on my way home from a business trip. I opened my Bible and landed in Ezekiel 37. I saw this passage of Scripture in an entirely new light, which I talked about in chapter 4. I flipped back in my Bible to read the chapters leading up to Ezekiel 37. There it was, bold yet hidden: "So I will rescue my flock, and they will no longer be abused" (Ezekiel 34:22). Then starting in verse 25, Ezekiel talked about the restoration of the abused! There are many other passages in the Bible on the restoration of the abused, including Isaiah 43, 55, 61; Jeremiah 31; and Hosea 2:14–19.

Abuse is sprinkled throughout Scripture, but we rarely hear sermons about it. Israel was trapped in abuse for around four hundred years. Abigail was abused by her husband, Nabal. King Saul abused David. Ammon abused his sister Tamar, and Absalom retraumatized her. The Midianites abused Israel in Judges 6, stealing, tormenting, and killing because they were too lazy to grow their own food. Sarah abused Hagar, banishing her to the desert to die with her son. Jeremiah was abused for preaching the message God gave him. Jesus was horrifically abused in the hours leading to his death.

The most overlooked verse on abuse is recorded in Malachi 2:16: "'For I hate divorce!' says the LORD, the God of Israel. 'To divorce your wife is to overwhelm her with cruelty,' says the LORD of Heaven's Armies. 'So guard your heart; do not be unfaithful to your wife.'"

As Christians we tend to believe that God puts his hate of divorce above people, but that is so far from the truth. "To divorce your wife is to overwhelm her with cruelty." The word *cruelty* means "violence, a strong, fierce, destructive force resulting in acts that maim, destroy, kill, often implying a lawlessness, terror and lack of moral restraint."[8]

These men were tossing their wife out of their home, without a legal divorce, and with no way to support themselves, which is violent and cruel. I'm not debating or defending divorce. If you would like to study this topic more, you can find two resources on the biblical study of divorce in the endnotes.[9]

Paul had much to say about abusive behavior in Ephesians 4:18–19: "Their minds are full of darkness; they wander far from the life God gives because they have closed their minds and hardened their hearts against him. They have no sense of shame. They live for lustful pleasure and eagerly practice every kind of impurity."

David says it this way in Psalm 36:1–4: "They have no fear of God at all. In their blind conceit, they cannot see how wicked they really are. Everything they say is crooked and deceitful. They refuse to act wisely or do good. They lie awake at night, hatching sinful plots. Their actions are never good. They make no attempt to turn from evil."

This is a graphic descriptions of an abuser. I'm often asked, Why doesn't the abuser repent or see what he's doing? Most times it's because he doesn't think he's done anything wrong so he has no need to repent. Ever the victim or the hero, he will never admit to being the villain. "But can't God change him?" He can. After all, he's God, he's all-powerful, he can do anything. The one thing God can do but won't is violate our free will. He won't force people to choose him.

The belief that God is in control has led us to believe that he'll keep bad things from happening to us. Sometimes he does, but many times he doesn't. Why? I do not know. The Bible is full of stories of injustice beginning with Cain and Abel. Even though God may not stop abusers from abusing, he always provides the abuser a way out, if they choose it. Too often they don't. Looking back, I can see all the times God gave Guy the opportunity to turn to him.

In chapter 1, I shared about our twenty-ninth wedding anniversary. Guy told me later that when he came home from patrolling, his intent was to wake me up so we could talk. Guy said he wasn't sure what happened, but I know he chose violence over talking.

Paul describes it this way, "The temptations in your life are no different from what others experience. And God is faithful. He will not allow the temptation to be more than you can stand. When you are tempted, he will show you a way out so that you can endure" (1 Corinthians 10:13). The question is whether the abuser takes advantage of the "way out." He has a choice to abuse or not. Most abusers say they don't have a choice, that they can't control it. Yet they are purposeful in all they do to harm with words or fists.

I felt sad when one woman shared with me her story about her pastor, who said abuse isn't in the Bible. It's as if he never read his Bible. Abuse is *all over* the Bible. Just read about Joseph in Genesis 37, and how he was abused by his own brothers.

Paul had much to say to the early church about abusive behaviors, and he should know. Paul was an abuser, himself. He also believed he was doing God's will when he killed Christ followers.

Ephesians 4:29–32, 5:3–4, and Colossians 3:5–11 list the abusive behaviors we must stop:

- Stop telling lies.
- Don't let anger control you.
- Stop stealing.
- Don't use foul or abusive words.
- Don't bring sorrow by the way you live.
- Get rid of all bitterness, rage, anger, harsh words, slander and all evil behavior.
- Have nothing to do with sexual immorality, impurity, lust, and evil desires.
- Reject sexual immorality, impurity, or greed.
- Stop using obscene stories, foolish talk, and coarse jokes.
- Don't be greedy.
- Get rid of anger, rage, malicious behavior, slander, and dirty language.
- Don't lie.
- Put off all wicked deeds.

Paul challenged us to put off and get rid of all these behaviors. Paul went so far as to say, "You can be sure that no immoral, impure, or greedy person will inherit the Kingdom of Christ and of God"

(Ephesians 5:5). Paul went on to challenge believers in verse 6: "Don't be fooled by those who try to excuse these sins, for the anger of God will fall on all who disobey him."

Were you like me and never read these verses as a description of abusers? It's so obvious, yet many in the church don't want to believe that people who talk about Jesus are actually evil. Or they want to believe that everyone who attends church is saved.

I can't say it enough—God does not condone abuse. Abuse isn't a marriage issue and can't be solved through marriage counseling. It is an individual issue that is evidenced in one's life long before marriage. Does Jesus abuse his church? Of course not. That's ridiculous to even say. Yet listen to the biblical standard for how a man should love his wife:

> The husband provides leadership to his wife the way Christ does to his church, not by domineering but by cherishing. . . . Husbands, go all out in your love for your wives, exactly as Christ did for the church—a love marked by giving, not getting. Christ's love makes the church whole. His words evoke her beauty. Everything he does and says is designed to bring the best out of her, dressing her is dazzling white silk, radiant with holiness. And that is how husbands ought to love their wives. (Ephesians 5:23, 25–28 MSG)

None of Paul's words imply that abuse of any kind is okay with God, Jesus, or the Holy Spirit. How do we as the body of Christ overlook abuse, refusing to believe her because he doesn't *look* like an abuser, or shunning her when she seeks a divorce and refuses to return to him because he apologized?

BeLoved, I'm so sorry some in my church hurt you, shunned you, and drove you from me. Come to me, my darling. I will save you, set you free, heal you, and redeem you.

~Your loving Husband, Jesus

WHAT CAN THE CHURCH DO?

When did a wife become responsible for her husband's behavior and keeping the marriage together? When did it become okay for men to harm the family and for women to be blamed? When did the church abdicate its role to protect women and children in order to protect marriage? These are questions I had no answers for, so I asked the one who does.

It started with Adam in Genesis 3, when he blamed the woman God gave him as the reason he ate the forbidden fruit. He said it wasn't his fault, it was hers; he wouldn't have eaten if she hadn't offered it. Here we are thousands of years later, and women are still blamed for choices men make.

Many churches are educated and informed on how to handle domestic violence. And many churches aren't educated nor are they informed on how to help women and children or how to recognize abuse versus a couple having marital problems. Ministries exist to educate pastors, elders, and leaders in the church about domestic violence.[10]

My hope is that this book will make it into churches so leaders can give it to women whom they aren't equipped to help. This chapter is more for church leadership, though I hope as you read the stories I gathered, you will know you aren't alone.

I gathered stories from across the country of women of all ages, churches, and beliefs. Here are portions of their stories of what happened when they sought help from church leaders, and what they wish had happened when they went to their churches for help.

L'S STORY

"We'd been married for a couple years. He was angry and one day used physical force. I went to our pastor's home. They offered me a couple days of safety. His counsel was to tell me that is the kind of behavior that is pretty common in the church, not much to be upset about. I should go back to my husband, and we should both be less selfish.

"Years later I sought help in our next church. We counseled with an older couple who reported to the pastor. Their advice to my husband was to buy me more presents, spend more time with the kids. Their advice to me was to stop being rebellious and find ways to accommodate my husband's frequent anger and constant travel. In short, I was told to forgive his rage faster, accommodate his behavior, and give him more sex. This is how a Christian woman behaves toward her husband.

"What I needed to hear was that I didn't deserve physical or emotional abuse. I needed help finding safe shelter while my husband went through effective intervention to deal with the cause of his rage. I needed to hear that accommodating bad behavior in the name of love isn't love for either of us. I needed to know I wasn't to blame and I needed help to find someone to confide in and help for restoration."

N'S STORY

"I tried telling the pastor—isn't he supposed to be a safe haven of trust? He counseled my husband, who lied so well that the pastor called me in and said I contributed to my husband's anger because I pushed his buttons and knew what I was doing. In the pastor's eyes, I was the one starting the violence by verbally provoking my husband to hit me! I thought, *Wonder if he's right?* So I stayed. The physical abuse continued. Years later I left when my husband was out of town. I sought a divorce, thinking I would be free, but the whole church shunned me. I was told I was going to hell because I was seeking the divorce, and that a woman can't seek a divorce unless adultery is proven. I was told my divorce wouldn't be valid in God's eyes, and even if I did prove adultery, I was still wrong, to the point I could never marry again because I'd be an adulteress and make the one I married an adulterer.

"My husband spread rumors that I was having affairs and that he was in the right. Since he was a youth leader, no one would believe he could do what I said he did. There is so much more.

"What do I wish would have happened? I wish the church would listen and help women get the help they need to get out, help them get proof of domestic violence, help with doctor visits, do whatever is needed to cast out the wolves dressed in sheep's clothing."

S'S STORY

"I was told: 'God hates divorce. Leave for your safety, it's your responsibility for your children's safety, but don't divorce him or go through the courts for child support.' This was in the 90s.

"In the mid-2000s I was told I needed to honor and respect my husband, regarding mistreatment, abusive treatment, and drinking, and to not push him. I was told I should allow God to convict him, and that it's not my job. In 2018, I was told in reference to his sex addiction, I should pray more, fast, intercede in the courts of heaven, and was actually asked by a female pastor, 'Well, why don't you want to have sex with him?' She also told me not to correct my husband, because that is the church's job or God's."

TOO MANY STORIES

I wish there weren't so many stories of poor advice and critical judgment from the church toward women seeking help from their abusive marriages. Here are a few more responses from hurting women who sought help from their church but were shamed instead:

- "I was told, 'Divorce should never have been your first stop.'"
- "I was asked, 'Don't you want to glorify God with your marriage?'"
- "He was believed because he put on such a good act."
- "I was believed, but then they didn't want to talk behind my elder-husband's back."
- "I was *in sin* because I wouldn't let my abusive husband come

home, and I was disobedient because *delayed obedience* is disobedience."

- "I was told not to use the word *abuse*, because it would upset my husband."
- "They acknowledged my husband was abusive and wanted us to attend marriage counseling, treating it as a marriage issue."
- "This church had no framework for distinguishing abuse from any other marriage problem."
- "I was told I was not righteous and [was] reaping the consequences of my own sin."
- "My husband repented of some of his issues to our pastor, who then thought I'd overacted."
- "They would not support legal separation in spite of adultery, I could never remarry, and I was given judgment without love."

Too often the abusive husband is believed as he spins his tale of woe about how hard it is to live with his wife. "It's all in her head." "She's not herself. I didn't do whatever she said I did." Or when he says, "I'm sorry," church leaders determine she should take him back. The wife is shamed for not being enough for her husband. She is retraumatized by the leaders in the church when she reaches out for help.

Isn't it sad that women are required to prove to leaders and the courts that they've been abused, and all he has to say is, "I didn't do it"? He is believed, while she is shamed for not being a good wife.

Again, abuse isn't a marriage problem and can't be fixed by marriage counseling. Marriage counseling assumes both are at fault and have issues each must work through. Abusive behavior is an individual issue which only the *abuser* can resolve. The abused can do nothing to make her abuser a better man or husband.

Based on the stories in the Gospels, Jesus held women and children in high regard. He said anyone who would harm a child should be drowned (Luke 17:2). Harsh.

As a church, we long to share Jesus with those who don't know him. We give to missions, help the poor. But what about helping the hurting women within our churches who are being battered and abused by their husbands?

Church, we must do better. We need to be a safe place for women and children, and we need to stop telling wives to be better and start challenging men who are abusive and violent.

LET ME TELL YOU A STORY

Imagine you're a businessman walking to his car after a late dinner, and out of nowhere, a big bully of a man blocks your path. You quickly look around, realizing you're alone. The bully demands your money and valuables, but it isn't enough, so he drags you into an alley and proceeds to pummel you with fists, kicking, slamming your head into the ground until you think you're going to die. All the while he berates you, calling you a worthless piece of manhood, gutless, powerless, spineless. Left for dead, you beg God to help you.

Barely alive, you're rushed to the hospital. Through your pain and agony, the doctors and nurses ask, "Why did he allow this to happen? I wonder what he did to cause this?" When the nurse comes in to check on your condition, you can feel her distain as she wonders what you did to cause the other man to rob and beat you as he did.

The attacker is caught, and during the trial his lawyer blames you for being in the wrong place. If only you had more money on you, he wouldn't have attacked you. You shouldn't have been out after dark, you should have worn a cheaper suit, and the list goes on. Your attacker's behaviors are excused while you are interrogated as if you're the one who could have stopped the attack in the first place.

The judge listens to both sides, then tells you to forgive him since the attacker said, "I'm sorry." Further, you should show him kindness by allowing him to move into your home so you can love your attacker. You are told to be kind to him, because maybe he'll change. After all, this is your fault for not being a good enough man. You wouldn't have been attacked if you weren't out after dark. And he can't be *that* bad. Look at him, he's calm and well-spoken. He doesn't look like a bully.

This may sound extreme, but this is what happens in too many churches and courtrooms when women seek help from abuse. Women aren't believed and are told they are exaggerating what happened. And the Lord is using the abuser, so he can't be as bad as you said. After all, he's an elder, deacon, pastor, lay leader, youth leader, businessman, police officer, and so on. Pick any career because abuse impacts almost every society and nation.

As the body of Christ, we don't want to believe wolves are hiding in our church. Jeremiah 12:2 says, "Your name is on their lips, but you are far from their hearts." We assume because they say the right words, people know Jesus, that the image they present is who they truly are. And we couldn't be more wrong.

WHAT CAN THE CHURCH DO TO HELP?

Listen to the woman seeking help. Talking to you is hard for her. She feels exposed and ashamed. Part of her believes she's at fault. She's terrified of him, and she's unsure how he'll respond and what he will do. Believe her. As outrageous as her story sounds, she's not exaggerating. If anything, she's downplaying how bad it is. Show her compassion and love. Be careful of your facial expressions—your face says so much more than your words. Console and reassure her that it's not her fault.

She's not complaining about her husband, and she didn't do anything wrong. She didn't make him do it. He didn't have a bad day at the office. Don't downplay the violence, even if he didn't hit her. Trust me when I tell you that verbal and emotional abuse are just as violent as getting hit.

Before confronting him, you must know the signs of an abuser. Abusers are adept at spinning tales to make themselves look right. She will be hysterical and unbalanced; he'll be calm and shocked that you would listen to her or think that he could do such horrific things.

Help her find a safe place if she's ready to leave him. If she's not ready to leave, then do not under any circumstances talk to her husband. If you do, you are putting her and the children in danger. Don't suggest marriage counseling; it's not a marriage problem. Help her find a counselor who understands trauma and abuse so she can get some help.

If you don't know how to help, reach out to a local shelter that can advise you. Educate yourself by reading *Mending the Soul* by Steven R. Tracy and *The Heart of Domestic Abuse* by Rev. Chris Moles. You will learn more than you ever wanted to know about what abusers look like. You will be horrified that anyone could be so evil and attend church. *Peace Works* by Rev. Chris Moles is another resource to show you how to help the women and children in your care.

Evil resides in our churches, only it looks normal. It quotes Scripture, prays, and serves in church. Abusers are charismatic and smooth talkers. Paul warns us in Ephesians 5:6, "Don't be fooled by those who try to excuse these sins." And in Titus 1:16, "Such people claim they know God, but they deny him by the way they live. They are detestable and disobedient, worthless for doing anything good."

If you're still not sure, ask Jesus to dispel the darkness, remove the veil, and give you eyes to see beyond the words they are speaking and ears to hear the difference between truth and lies.

Thank you, Pastor, for listening and being willing to see another side of life that we wish didn't exist.

SAY THIS, NOT THAT

This section is for family and friends, most of whom said all the wrong things to you when you chose to leave your abuser. These are some of the things you might hear from well-intentioned family and friends:

- I wouldn't put up with that for five minutes.
- I'm not sure who I'm more mad at: you for staying or him for what he did to you.
- You need to move on or get over it.
- Let me tell you what happened to me.
- Are you sure it's that bad?
- He's so nice and well respected in the community.
- I told you not to marry him.
- You looked like the perfect family.
- What was your part? It takes two to tango.
- If you remarry, you'll be committing adultery.

BELIEVE HER

She's not complaining about her husband, she is sharing her deepest, darkest secrets, letting you into her nightmare. Talking to you is her act of bravery, though to her it doesn't feel brave, it feels terrifying. Her story will sound outrageous and unbelievable and she hasn't yet shared her worst moments.

DON'T GIVE ADVICE

Avoid asking questions and giving advice; just listen. Unless you've experienced domestic violence, you can't know what she is feeling. Your advice may do more harm than good. If you don't know what to say, say nothing. Instead, love and comfort her.

DON'T DOWNPLAY HIS ACTIONS

Don't make excuses for him, implying he didn't mean it, or saying something condescending like, "At least he didn't hit you." Non-physical violence can be more harmful than physical violence, since it strips her of her identity and is actually brainwashing her. It leaves wounds you can't see, but you can hear if you listen.

DON'T JUDGE

Avoid judgment of either her and him. If you think you know him, you don't. It will be hard to imagine with what you do know about him that he could be capable of such evil. Our facial expressions can covey the opposite of what our words say. On the inside you may be horrified, but your face should show compassion and caring.

DON'T ASSUME SHE PROVOKED HIM

In marriage we assume it takes two to fight. In a non-abusive marriage it is true but in an abusive marriage it isn't true at all. She may believe that she abuses him too. She may think that she is partly responsible or fully responsible: if only she hadn't done this or that or if she'd done something different, he wouldn't have reacted.

She has no idea that he's blamed her and made her responsible for his behavior. It's a tactic that starts early in the marriage and likely while they dated. She may have no idea that he's conditioned her to respond to him in certain ways.

She's trapped in his deception, so go easy on her. She can't see clearly. Whether she knows it or not, she lives in a constant state of fear.

DON'T PRESSURE HER TO LEAVE

If she's not ready to leave, don't pressure her, even if you're terrified for her safety. It will simply lead to more anxiety for her. Only she can choose to leave. She needs to come to her defining moment— the moment she realizes she's done and doesn't want to live this way anymore. Even when she makes this decision, it may take time for her to act on her decision.

Fear is driving her, though she may not know it. She will second-guess every choice she makes, including the choice to leave.

WHAT CAN YOU DO?

Love and believe her. I can't say this enough: our biggest fear is that we won't be believed. He has created a cone of silence around his family, warning her about ruining his name and his career.

Learn about the dynamics of abuse and narcissistic abuse. The more you know, the more understanding you can be. Be empathetic but don't take on her burden; it will be too heavy for you and may even trigger any unhealed wounds you have. At times she'll be irrational and seem unbalanced. It will drain you, and most people can't handle her pain and will abandon her.

DO OFFER HELP

If you sense that something isn't right in her marriage, you can tell her if she ever needs help that you are there for her. If she does tell you, let her know she's safe, and if she needs a soft place to land you will help her in any way you can. Don't give her money or books that she might have to explain to him. Show her how to go online to sites about abuse. Every site has an escape feature.

PROVIDE TANGIBLE HELP

She may have left with the clothes on her back and no money, so provide her with practical necessities like meals, gift cards, groceries, clothes for her and her children if she has kids. Help her find a safe place to live, babysit for her so she can look for a job, take her to get a manicure and pedicure or get her hair done. Spoil and love her with more than words. Support her, hug her, don't ask her to explain or to justify why she left.

HELP HER PLAN

When she's ready to leave, help her plan. Offer to keep her important papers and cash, help her open a checking account, let her use your mailing address. And most important, help her find a place to stay besides your house. She needs a place where he can't find her.

Help her check her phone for tracking apps or help her get a flip phone that can't be tracked. Remind her not to tell him she's leaving. This is the most dangerous moment for her. Even if he's not physically violent, that's no guarantee he won't become that way when she leaves him.

Help her find an attorney. Most attorneys provide a thirty-minute free consultation. She can learn her rights and expectations if or when she decides to file.

Let her text you and remind her to delete her texts. Offer to save the text messages for her as evidence. She's not being deceptive. She's being safe.

The best advice I can give is if you don't know what to do, learn all you can about abuse before you approach her. If she comes to you, it's because she believes you're trustworthy.

ACKNOWLEDGMENTS

My deepest appreciation to the women who prayed me through this book: Lynda, Ellen, Martha, Judy, and many others who encouraged me to keep writing.

Cindi McMenamin, for your constant encouragement and coaching me through the writing, telling me the hard truth, reminding me this book isn't about me but the women who will read it.

My Living Write Texas tribe—Deb, Michele, Sharon, Lori, René, Leslie, Donna, Michelle, and Laura. You are fabulous writers and encouragers.

My agent, Cyle Young, who gave this newbie a chance. Catherine DeVries from Kregel, who listened to my pitch and saw the potential of my book.

My brave mommy, Virginia Rolin, my Moses who rescued me and helped me when I couldn't help myself. My family who surrounded, loved, and helped me when I couldn't help myself.

Tom Gardner, my husband, friend, and bodyguard—you are my kinsman-redeemer. You taught me how to love and be loved.

My children, who as adults have helped me become a better mom.

Thank you to each and every reader. My hope is that this book helped you as much as it did me, as I recorded all God did in my life and will do in yours.

Last but not least, Jesus, who loved and pursued this shattered sixteen-year-old who thought she was unlovable and unworthy. He drew me in and never let me go as I healed from the trauma of domestic violence. He constantly reminds me that I can do anything through him, and he is my strength and my rock-solid wall.

You can connect with me at AnotherOneFree.com or at Karen DeArmondGardner.com. I would be honored if you'd sign up for my email newsletter to stay connected and receive updates of future books and encouragement.

If you have further questions or just want someone to listen, email me at Karen@AnotherOneFree.com.

I'm also on Facebook (Another One Free) and Instagram (@karen gardnerauthor).

NOTES

1. James Strong, *The New Strong's Complete Dictionary of Bible Words* (Nashville: Thomas Nelson, 1996).
2. Corrie Cutrer, "The Silent Epidemic," *Today's Christian Woman*, September 2004, https://www.todayschristianwoman.com/articles /2004/September/silent-epidemic.html.
3. "Brain Areas and Their Functions," Health24, September 2, 2011, https://m.health24.com/Mental-Health/Brain/Anatomy-of-the -brain/Brain-areas-and-their-functions-20120721.
4. Francis Brown, S. R. Driver, and Charles A. Briggs, *The Enhanced Brown-Driver-Briggs Hebrew and English Lexicon* (Oxford: Clarendon Press, 1977).
5. "What Is Coercive Control in a Relationship?," WebMd, May 23, 2017, https://www.webmd.com/women/features/what-is-coercive -control#1. See also "What Is Coercive Control?," Neurotypical Site, 2011, https://www.theneurotypical.com/coercive-control.html; and "Beyond Physical Violence: What Is Coercive Control?," House of Peace Virtual Training Center, December 28, 2018, https://houseofpeacepubs.com/wordpress/beyond-physical-violence -what-is-coercive-control/.
6. Power and Control Wheel (Duluth, MN: Domestic Abuse Intervention Programs, 2017), https://www.theduluthmodel.org /wp-content/uploads/2017/03/PowerandControl.pdf. Used with permission. For more information, contact Domestic Abuse Intervention Programs, 202 East Superior Street, Duluth, MN, 55802. 218-722-2781. www.theduluthmodel.org.
7. WordReference.com, s.v. "Stockholm syndrome," accessed April 2, 2021, https://www.wordreference.com/definition/Stockholm%20 syndrome.
8. James A. Swanson, *Dictionary of Biblical Languages with Semantic Domains: Hebrew* (Bellingham, WA: FaithLife, 2002).
9. Paul Blue, "Divorce in the Old Testament," ChangeMyRelation

ship.com, 2010, https://karladowningresources.files.wordpress.com/2011/05/divorce_in_the_old_testament.pdf. See also Herbert Vander Lugt, "Divorce and Remarriage: What Does the Bible Teach?," Our Daily Bread Ministries, accessed April 2, 2021, https://discoveryseries.org/courses/divorce-and-remarriage/.

10. Pastor Chris Moles runs the ministry PeaceWorks; find out more at www.chrismoles.org. See also Leslie Vernick at leslievernick.com.